THE CUCI

A Sussex

A Journey from its source
to the sea

From small beginnings – one of the source streams above Horsebridge.

Ann Botha

S.B. Publications

By the same author
The Crumbles Story

*To my parents
who loved the Cuckmere*

First published in 2000 by S. B. Publications,
19 Grove Road, Seaford, East Sussex BN25 1TP

ISBN 1 85770 189 5

Designed and typeset by CGB, Lewes
Printed by Tansleys The Printers
19 Broad Street, Seaford, East Sussex BN25 1LS

CONTENTS

ACKNOWLEDGEMENTS

The author is indebted to the many people who have given her insight and information about the river and the countryside through which it flows. These include Brian Deeprose of the Rivers Authority branch of the Environment Agency, who provided a wealth of information and maps of the river; Andrew Beattie, Head Ranger of the Seven Sisters Country Park; Roy Pryce; Peter Hay; and the Merrydown Wine Company. The staff in the reference section of Eastbourne and Heathfield branch libraries were most helpful and Sharon Searle generously shared her own extensive writings and knowledge of the area.

The owners of both Heathfield Park and Charleston Manor kindly allowed the author to visit their properties and photograph them and Jim Wilson, the Estate Manager at Heathfield Park and Peter Wesson at Charleston gave their valuable time for an unforgettable and informative tour on each occasion. St Bede's School kindly provided a picture of Horatio Bottomley's country house and gave permission for its reproduction. All other photographs are by the author except where otherwise indicated in the captions.

Finally, the author and the publisher owe a particular debt of gratitude to the late Edna and 'Mac' McCarthy, whose *The Cuckmere – Another Sussex River*, first published in 1981 and now sadly out of print, was the inspiration for this book, and who kindly gave permission for the use of maps and illustrations from their original publication.

INTRODUCTION

The chalk hills of the South Downs stretch for some eighty miles from Beachy Head in the east to the Hampshire border in the west and are the most striking natural feature of Sussex. These green rolling contours have an average width of five miles and the southern slopes are gentle and marked by dry valleys which are unable to hold water for the chalk itself is porous. A coastal plain in the west between the Downs and the sea ends at Brighton and from Black Rock the southern slopes meet the sea, where centuries of erosion have carved sheer white cliffs which now extend eastwards to the end of the range.

The northern slopes are steep, forming an escarpment which can reach 800 feet and it is from these heights that the panorama of the Weald unfolds far below and away to the edge of the North Downs. This gently undulating countryside was once an area of almost impenetrable forest, named by the Celts *Andred* and by the Anglo Saxons the *Wyld*. Now it is mainly farmland and though there are towns they are lost to sight in the great distances to be seen from the Downs. Cutting across the Weald are higher ridges of land and it is here that remnants of the ancient forest still exist.

This then is the setting for the four main rivers of Sussex which rise in the Weald and flow to the sea through valleys in the chalk hills. From west to east they are the Arun, the Adur, the Ouse and the Cuckmere. All have their own charm but the smallest river, the Cuckmere, is unlike the others for it has no town or port at its entrance to the sea. It is named from the Saxon *cwicu mere*, which means living or fast flowing water and the valley that it cuts through the Downs has the majestic Windover and Hindover hills on each side and is a place of great natural beauty. From source to sea the river follows a course that passes through fields and woods, touching here and there the small towns and villages which are the very essence of Sussex.

This most gentle of rivers has a past rich in history. Let us trace that past from the source streams to the sea, discovering the natural and man made changes that have taken place over the centuries.

Ann Botha
Eastbourne

5

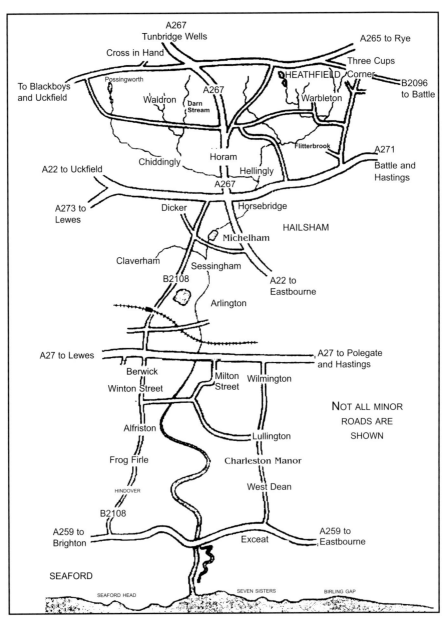

Sketch map showing the course of the Cuckmere and the regions featured in the text.

The Heathfield ridge, which rises some 500ft above sea level, seen on the horizon across the Vale of Sussex.

1

THE JOURNEY BEGINS

Looking north across the Vale of Sussex from the slopes of Windover hill a line of hills can be clearly seen, smudged to a hazy blue on the horizon. These are at the southern edge of the High Weald, an area of gently rolling ridges and steep valleys, which extends across parts of East and West Sussex, Kent and Surrey. Between the villages and towns are large tracts of countryside – a place of fields, thick hedgerows and extensive woodlands, echoes of the ancient forest which once dominated the area. The High Weald is the least known of the forty one sites in England and Wales designated as Areas of Outstanding Natural Beauty (AONB) and retains an atmosphere of quiet remoteness.

The geology of Sussex is generally speaking neatly divided into areas of chalk on the Downs, clay and silt in the low areas of the Weald, and hard sandstone, shale and limestone on the High Weald. It is here on the southern slopes of the hills close to where the A265 passes along the

Sunlight speckles the waters of the rust red Flitterbrook as it flows through a wooded valley at Rushlake Green.

ridgeway through Heathfield that the small streams and headwaters of the Cuckmere begin their journey south.

The source streams

To the west, the headwaters rise in Possingworth Park beyond Cross in Hand and to the east in Kemps Wood, near Three Cups Corner, its name deriving from the fact that three small rivers, the Cuckmere, Rother and Christians River, which joins the Ashburn, rise at this point. The principal stream of the Cuckmere rises in Heathfield Park, flows south to become the Vines Cross stream, links with streams from Warbleton and is joined by the Waldron Ghyll which begins its flow close to what was Heathfield station until the Cuckoo Line was closed. The Possingworth stream links with the Darn and the Summersbrook to become the Bull River flowing south where it is joined by the Chiddingly streams and then turns south east. Nine miles to the south, close to Horselunges Manor at Hellingly, the main sources come together to form the Cuckmere river.

This is an area perhaps little known by those who know the Cuckmere only in its lower valley reaches. The scenery at its source is entirely different. It is a place of narrow shady lanes, with clusters of timber framed cottages, many originally with thatched roofs, and the handsome larger houses that sixteenth century and later landowners had built of stone and tile.

To the east, near Three Cups Corner where the cheekily named Flitterbrook rises in Kemps Wood, the road leads south to Rushlake Green where houses stand round a triangular green and on the western side the ground slopes down to a small steep valley. South of the green a swing gate leads to a footpath and a small plate on this gate marks a modern tragedy, for near here Ian Price was killed while repairing power lines after the hurricane of 1987. Follow the path downhill into the thickly wooded valley and here a small bridge crosses the Flitterbrook, full and swift flowing after rains.

This tranquil place is typical of so many of the valleys where streams pass under small bridges all along these slopes. Cool and shaded, the sunlight shafts down through the trees and the only sounds heard are bird song, the stirring of leaves and the running water. It was not always so, for here, between the fifteenth and eighteenth centuries, the small

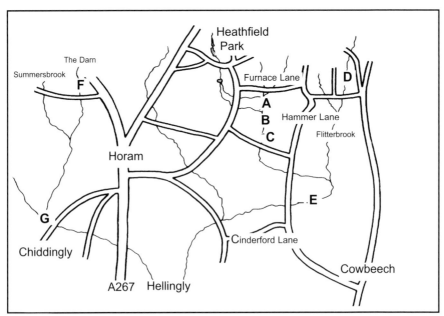

Sketch map of sites of former iron mills in the upper reaches of the Cuckmere.
A: Heathfield Furnace. B: Woodmans Furnace. C: Steel Forge. D: Markly or
Rushlake Green Furnace. E: Cradle Furnace and Forge. F: Waldron Furnace.
G: Stream Furnace and Forge, Chiddingly.

rushing streams of the Cuckmere headwaters provided power for the
iron industry which flourished in this area. A little further upstream is
an old pond bay – all that is now left of the old Markly or Rushlake
Green furnace.

The iron industry

From before the Roman occupation there is evidence that there was an
iron industry of some sort in the Weald where the necessary raw mate-
rial was to be found in nodules close to the surface in the beds of
Wadhurst clay. The methods of production were simple. A small furnace
or hearth was built, made of alternate layers of charcoal and iron ore,
and once the fire was kindled the furnace was closed, often covered by
clay, and bellows made from animal skins kept the heat at a high tem-
perature. This produced from rich ore a lump of malleable iron which at

that stage was not pure as it contained cinder which had to be beaten out. Hammered into a solid mass, this was later called a bloom, a term derived from the Saxon word *bloma* and the phrase *bloma ferri* is recorded in the Domesday Book. Bellows were not a new idea as they had been used in the working of gold, silver and copper before iron was known, but these first bloomeries were sited in valleys by streams, the water being used for cooling the tools.

Two innovations from the Continent, the water-powered bloomery forge and the blast furnace, turned a local industry into big business in the fifteenth century. These later furnaces were also sited by streams so that when the furnace was closed large wooden water wheels supplied power to the bellows to keep the heat in blast for several hours. Dams were built across the streams to form a pond bay so that water could be allowed to flood through with enough force to keep the water wheels turning, giving power first to the furnace and then the great hammers of the forge.

Warbleton

From Rushlake Green the road leads west to Warbleton, a village named after *Wealdburh*, one of the few Saxon women to have owned land in the county. The feeling of centuries long gone is strong in this remote corner of Sussex. The village inn, which was called the Two Tuns in 1690, acquired its punning name of the Warbill in Tun much later. The inn is part of a small cluster of houses lining one side of the road which leads up to a farm and the Church of St Mary the Virgin, built on the raised ground of a Neolithic earthwork. This fine church has two thirteenth century windows and a galleried manorial pew which was built in 1722 to give the lord of the manor and his family and friends an elevated position above the congregation and an excellent view of the chancel and pulpit.

Richard Woodman – ironmaster and martyr

Nearby, footpaths descend through Causeway Wood on the west of Hammer Lane to the pond bays of Woodman's Furnace and Steel Forge which were powered by the waters of the Flitterbrook. Water was allowed to flood through the earthen dams across the stream to turn the

The churchyard lych gate and the old houses with their peg tiled roofs that line the road through Warbleton. Below, the memorial to Richard Woodman.

1888

CLOSE BY,
IN
THE MEADOW
BEHIND,
STOOD THE
ABODE OF
RICHARD
WOODMAN,
FARMER AND
IRON-MASTER,
BURNT AT
LEWES
22 JUNE 1557.

wheels that supplied the power to forge or furnace, either to work the giant bellows or drive the great tilt hammers used to produce wrought iron. Richard Woodman, the owner of the furnace and forge, was a farmer turned ironmaster and churchwarden of St Mary's. He met a tragic end, not by accident but very much by design. He had dared to call the rector, the Rev George Fayrebank, who had been a Protestant under Henry VIII but became a Roman Catholic in the reign of Queen Mary, 'Mr. Facing Both Ways' and paid with his life for this statement.

He had, at the age of thirty three, already spent two years of his life in prison for his religious beliefs and, brave and stubborn, he continued openly to oppose forced conversion to the Roman Catholic faith.

He was arrested, after escaping from, some say, the tower loft of the church. Another tradition is that he was fleeing from a secret chamber in his house, which lay just south of the church, when it was surrounded by the sheriff's men. Before his trial he wrote an account of what happened when he ran away and this gives credence to him hiding in the church tower, for he says he had:

> '. . . leaped down, having no shoes on. So I took down a lane ful of sharp synders, and they came running after with a great cry, with their swords drawn, crying Strike him! Strike him!'

He was well ahead of his pursuers, he says, when he stepped on a sharp cinder and fell and before he could 'arise and get away he was come up to me.' And so the ironmaster was caught, brought down by the detritus of the industry at which he had made his living. During his trial Woodman asked to be allowed to return to his business on which the local workforce depended.

> 'Let me go home, I pray you, to my wife and children to see them kept and the poore folke that I would set aworke, a 100 persons ere this, all the yeare together.'

His dignified plea fell on deaf ears and the unfortunate man was burnt to death at the stake in Lewes on 22 June, 1557. During the five year reign of Mary Tudor more than 300 people were martyred for their religious beliefs and Richard Woodman's tragic part in this persecution is commemorated on the west wall of the nave of Warbleton Church and on a simple stone, pictured on facing page, set in the south wall of the churchyard.

2

WEAPONS OF WAR

Close to the main A265 road, which follows the ridgeway, are the extensive grounds of Heathfield Park. Here the main headwaters of the
Cuckmere spring from the ground and here, nearly 300 years ago, a
series of small lakes were made to serve one of John Fuller's iron furnaces and forge. The Fuller family were prosperous ironmasters who
had come from London in the last quarter of the sixteenth century when
John Fuller took over the lease of Tanners Manor at Waldron. In 1659 the
family purchased a large area of land, together with a mill, and in 1693
the Fullers increased their estates by purchasing land at Heathfield,
They then leased the Twissels mill in 1698 and bought Bayley Park (the
original name of Heathfield Park) in 1708.

Heathfield Furnace

The power of the main source stream from Heathfield Park, which
joined with two other streams to the east, must have been considerable
because below the Fuller's Heathfield furnace site near Nettlesworth
and Beckington bridges were two more iron workings – the Woodmans
furnace and below that, his Steel Forge.

Not only here along the southern slopes of the ridgeway on the sources
of the Cuckmere, but everywhere on the High Weald where iron was
mined and water power readily available, the iron industry grew in
importance from the fourteenth century onwards. From the time of
Henry VIII until the latter part of the eighteenth century the Weald had
a virtual monopoly in England in the manufacture of cast iron guns.

These weapons of war, notably heavy cannon for naval and military
use, became the main armaments for both defence and attack.
Gunpowder was the key which drove forward the invention of gun and

shot and though known to the Chinese long ago and also to the Greeks in a form called Greek fire, it was not used in Europe until the fourteenth century. An Elizabethan account in the British Museum darkly refers to 'the first invention of the Horryble Instrument of Gonnes' and goes on to describe the discovery of powder of brimstone and the striking of spark on stone to send a stone missile through the first guns. This took place in 1320, the invention of one 'Bertholdus Swartz, an Almayne, who taught it to the Venecians'. The historian ascribes the pipe of iron loaded with powder as a device by 'the Suggestion of the Devill himself.' A thought probably shared down the centuries by many as the ingenuity of the human brain and hand discovered yet more ways to defend or enlarge their territory, from the sling shot and spear to the horrors of nuclear war.

The casting of guns

The immorality of war and weapons cannot be denied but is a part of our history and the early guns were crude affairs of wrought iron bars welded together. The bloomery process produced only wrought iron, which in medieval times was a costly commodity, carefully husbanded by stewards of the manors, and worked up by the blacksmiths for the more peaceful purposes of agriculture and other uses.

In the fourteenth century there were also 'brass' or bronze guns, made of an alloy of copper or zinc. By the fifteenth century large iron guns were being made for siege purposes. Breech-loaded with stone shot, these were used by the English in the 1424 siege of Mont St Michel and in 1428 at Orleans. Later in the fifteenth century the French made even larger guns which fired balls of 15ins diameter, such as 'Mad Greta' of Ghent and the 'Mons Meg' of Edinburgh.

With the invention of the blast furnace, a process that was introduced from the Low Countries late in the fifteenth century, the iron industry on the High Weald became one of national importance. The ore was mined from pits ranging from 4ft to 40ft in depth. The furnace used then was a sandstone and brick built edifice of some height, fed at the open top by ore on to hot coals and the fluid metal tapped from an opening at the bottom. This could then be run into moulds or allowed to cool and heated again to acquire a plastic state and worked under the great hammers into bar iron.

First in a series of old feeder ponds in Heathfield Park and, below, one of the ponds that is now a large, tranquil lake.

These blast furnaces were fired for about two days before beginning the 'blow' from the large bellows and the parlance of 'foundays' meant six days, in which about eight tons of iron could be smelted. The hammers, which like the bellows were worked by water wheel, were used to beat out any remaining cinder or dross. Many of the smaller furnaces produced iron sows or pig iron, which was then sold on to London or larger foundries for further working. For these iron bars the melted ore was run into sand lined hollows.

The finer points in the process of gun founding which made the fortune of many ironmasters on the Weald were a jealously guarded secret but basically two methods were used. One was a mould, carefully constructed with a spindle of light wood which could be revolved and round which twisted bands of hay were wound in layers. The hay was coated with successive dressings of a mixture of clay, hair and manure to the required diameter, which was allowed to dry. The final coat of the mould was cut to the external shape of the finished gun and then coated with ash or butter to prevent adhesion. Iron hoops held the model firm before the final moulds of clay were added. Then the spindle was knocked out, leaving the hollow through the middle. Moulds of the breech end of the gun were made separately and attached to the model by wire. When all was ready the mould was lowered into a pit in front of the furnace and the molten metal run into it. These hollow cast guns were scraped clean inside by means of a riming tool, the gun casing being revolved by horse power. In a second later method the gun was cast solid and then bored through the hot metal with an iron rod wound with wire and coated with clay, a process used by the Fuller forge at Heathfield.

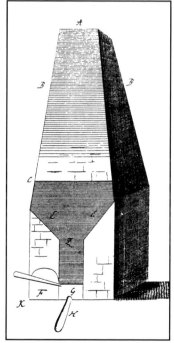

Engraving of a Wealden brick built blast furnace from Swedenborg's *De Ferro* of 1724.

The early large guns were named like ships but more general names for the type and size of guns were used in the sixteenth and seventeenth centuries. For example, Cannon Royal had a bore of 8.54 ins, weighed 8,000 lbs and the weight of shot was 74lbs. A Culverin gun had a bore of 5.2 ins, weighed 4,840 lbs, with shot of 18lbs, and at the bottom end of the scale a Robinet had a bore of only 1.01ins, weighed 300lbs and the shot weight was 0.3lbs. The cast iron gun on display at Pevensey Castle which is mounted on a modern reproduction carriage, is a Wealden Demi Culverin of the late sixteenth century with the cipher of Elizabeth I, a rose and crown with the initials E and R on each side. According to the Naval lists of the time a Demi Culverin had a bore of 40ins, weighed 3,400lbs, and the weight of the shot was 11lbs.

An inventory of ordnance artillery was made when in 1514 Henry VIII made peace with France and the 'Kynges Shippes' were laid up. Guns of all shapes and sizes were listed, and in the flagship, *Henry Grace de Dieu* there were twenty three brass guns and seventy three of iron. The *Mary Rose*, which was sunk at Portsmouth in 1545 and has since been recovered for restoration, had sixty guns in all.

These figures give some idea of the continuing need for bigger and better armaments and the landmark in the Sussex iron industry came in 1543 with the founding of the first cast iron gun at Buxted by Ralph Hogge and Peter Baude, a Frenchman, expert in the art.

The Fuller iron workings had a string of twelve feeder ponds running downstream for three miles to supply the pond bay at the Heathfield furnace. Here, and at other Fuller iron mills, cannon were cast and then sent to Woolwich for testing by the government before beginning their journey to places as far away as Ireland, Naples, Sicily and India. A large number of the population of Heathfield were employed in either furnace work, timber felling, haulage, charcoal burning or treading the wheel when the water flows were poor.

Accounts and records of 1739-40 show that 247 guns 'were made for the King'. Guns were cast for export too, the King of Sardinia ordering ninety, and these were 'proved' locally, a formal and splendid occasion for which the accounts show £20 for wine and £18 for the cook, which together with the costs of labour and powder amounted to a total of £180, no small sum in those days. With the firing of the cannon and the copious refreshment laid on for the buyers this must have been great fun, putting today's business lunches rather in the shade.

The late sixteenth century Wealden Demi Culverin at Pevensey Castle.

The Cuckmere could not be used for transporting these heavy goods and the guns were taken overland to the Medway or the Ouse, the Fuller records of June 1743 noting 'I have got twenty 9 pounders of 9 feet to Lewes and they are most of them on board the *Sussex Oak* which they promise to bring to Woolwich very speedily.' The record concludes with the wry information that 'These 20 have torn the roads so that nothing can follow them and the County curse us heartily.'

Ironmaster John Fuller

John Fuller was proud of the skills of his iron workers and said that 'only six furnaces in England can make great guns and one of them is at Heathfield'. The iron mills of the Weald were not in constant use, dependent as they were on the supply of ore and the varying water power according to season. In 1703 the Fuller furnace had twenty nine 'foundays' and in 1743 there were thirty five, each one lasting six days.

At the Fuller's Heathfield furnace the largest gun made was a 32-pounder Demy Cannon, 10 ft in length and weighing in total 6,384 lbs. The smaller furnaces, which were often leased by tenants, were useful for casting shot in addition to producing bar iron. Plenty of shot was required for the quantity of guns manufactured and in 1695 the ratio was recorded as 40 shot for heavy guns and 55 shot for lighter pieces.

Another variable in the industry was the supply of fuel. Wood for charcoal to feed the furnaces was as important as water and constant coppicing and felling gave rise to some concern. Sir John Pelham owned furnaces at Waldron and Brightling and the Pelham records show that many cords (1fl ton) of Copse Wood were required each year, ranging from a low figure of 597 in 1653, to 2,289 in 1655 for the Waldron furnace alone.

The arguments raged on for years about timber felling for the iron industry but Daniel Defoe, who toured the southern counties in 1724, wrote:

'I found this Complaint perfectly groundless, the three Counties of Kent, Sussex and Hampshire . . . being one inexhaustible Store-House of Timber.'

In fact, landowners were careful in their management of woodland and records state that coppices were cut every thirteen to seventeen years. A letter from John Fuller at Brightling in 1748 to a supplier of wood states:

Sir, You ask me advice about your Woods, you have had it over and over again; one of the Fellings was in 1735, the other in 1736, so one is thirteen years growth, the other twelve years; it will be time enough to bargain when the Woods are fellable which they are not now, nor will be in less than two years. . .'

So it seems with the obvious regard for sensible planting and felling that Daniel Defoe was right and the forests were well cared for.

The well kept records of the Fuller's furnaces give details of the finances of the business. For instance, in 1746 the Heathfield furnace total costs were £3,286 4s 0d which included ore, fuel, founders and casting, gun moulding labour and furnace wear and tear. The sales of iron brought in £5,466, ranging from £19 per ton down to £5 per ton, giving a profit of £2,179 16s 0d which in those days was well worth the having. Furnacemen earned 14s 0d for a 'founday', which was a working week of six days. Wages varied, with hammermen in 1539 earning 6s 8d per ton of bars, a piecework rate, rising to 7s 6d per ton in 1639. Woodcutters earned threepence per cord of wood and colliers 1s 10d per load.

A new fuel for the furnaces

By the mid eighteenth century gun founding at Heathfield had ceased but by that time the family's fortunes were made. The forges belonging to the Fullers and other prominent ironmasters turned to production of agricultural implements and domestic items such as andirons and firebacks. In the days when homes were warmed by wood or coal fires iron firebacks were popular and practical, often made for the larger houses of the gentlefolk in cast iron with illustrative designs in relief.

Fuller's Heathfield furnace closed completely in 1787. The demise of iron workings on the High Weald in the late eighteenth century was undoubtedly the result of the change from wood to coal as fuel for the blast furnaces. Inevitably the great iron mills and later the steel foundries of England became centred in the Midlands and the north where there were deposits of coal in quantity.

Today, on a small scale, echoes of the iron industry survive in Sussex. Charcoal is still produced in the region, providing the fuel for many a garden barbecue, using trees that have been felled for woodland management. Blacksmiths too are finding markets for ornamental ironwork, which has come back into fashion.

Many of the old pond bays and hammer ponds still exist and the names, too, are still here. Cinderford Lane, Hammer Lane, Furnace Lane, Furnace Wood, Cinder Brook, Smithland Wood and many more. A host of names which make it easy to imagine the cold rains and snow of the winter months when the streams were full and the men working in the iron foundries could break from their work to go outside for great lungfuls of fresh air and copious draughts of water.

Today the majority of the population of Sussex is mainly centred in the coastal towns, but once, and not so long ago, the iron ore held in the rich clay of the High Weald and the source streams of the Cuckmere and other rivers, made this region one of the most industrialised and important places in Britain.

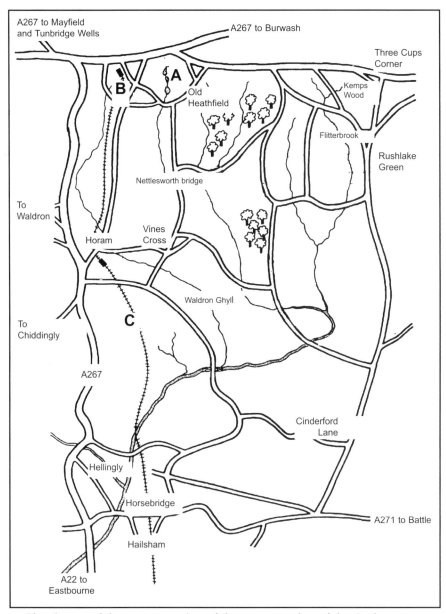

**Sketch map of the eastern section of the upper reaches of the Cuckmere.
A: Heathfield Park, B: Heathfield station. C: Cuckoo Line and Cuckoo Trail.**

3

HEATHFIELD AND THE PARK

All Saints and America

Before continuing west along the main A265 road a turn south from the B2096 Battle road follows the signs past the stone walls of Heathfield Park to Old Heathfield. Picturesque houses line the road to All Saints' church whch has an unusual stained glass window in the north wall. It shows Robert Hunt, a former vicar of Heathfield celebrating Holy Communion before a congregation of settlers and native Americans in Jamestown Virginia. This unexpected vision of America in a Sussex country church was given by Dawn Langley Simmons in memory of her grandmother and great aunt, who were twin sisters. It was unveiled by Dawn's adoptive mother, the celebrated English comedy actress, Dame Margaret Rutherford, in 1962.

The story depicted in glass is a true one, for in 1606 Robert Hunt sailed from London on the *Susan Constant II* bound for Virginia. After a long and stormy passage across the Atlantic he arrived safely to become the first Church of England minister to celebrate Holy Communion in what was to become the United States of America. His congregation of English settlers in Jamestown was small and in those pioneering days life was tough indeed. Robert Hunt himself survived for only a year. He is remembered not only in Sussex but also in Jamestown where a bronze bas-relief, consecrated in 1922, shows him conducting a service in his simple place of worship roofed by a sail.

Near the church in Old Heathfield is the Star Inn, parts of which date back 500 years. From its garden there is a view over woodlands to a lake fed by waters from two streams, one of which flows under Furnace Lane. Inside the inn, in 1830, there was a meeting that was to alter the

The Star Inn at Old Heathfield.

lives of some of the village's poorest inhabitants. The parish council agreed to give £291 to send fourteen adults and twenty two children to America. They were the first of some sixty inhabitants who emigrated in that year from the Heathfield area to try life in a new land.

The stone walls that surround Heathfield Park enclose 400 acres of ground and stretch for three and a half miles. Michael Harmer, brother of sculptor Jonathan Harmer, noted for his terra cotta plaques, started the wall Sir Charles Blunt had ordered in 1833 and finished it three years later.

General Elliot buys Bayly Park

After the Fuller family left Bayly Park, the 'Hero of the Rock' General George Augustus Elliot bought the estate in July 1766 for £4,000 as a country home for his family – the purchase price making only a tiny dent in the £24,000 prize money he had received for his successful campaigns in Cuba. Elliot became a national hero when the garrison he commanded successfully defended Gibraltar against the French and

Spanish from 1779 to 1783 in one of the greatest sieges in history. He was created Lord Heathfield of Gibraltar in 1787 and it was said of him that he ate only vegetables, drank only water and slept but four hours a night.

The Gibraltar Tower, in the north west corner of Heathfield Park, was built three years after the death of General Elliot by the new owner of the estate, Francis Newberry. He had bought the Park from Elliot's son and erected the 55ft high tower as a tribute to the General. The tower, which is 600ft above sea level, was gutted by fire in the Second World War. It was restored in the 1970s by Dr Gerald Moore as a feature of his Heathfield Wildlife Park and Gibraltar Tower Gardens – a popular tourist attraction which closed in 1981.

The Gibraltar Tower.

The house and grounds are the home of Norwegian shipping magnate Andreas Ugland and his family. He bought the eastern side of the park and the mansion in 1993 and three years later the remainder of the park, which includes the Gibraltar Tower.

The two springs that rise on the northern side of the grounds are the main source streams of the Cuckmere river. One is small, the rust coloured water flowing directly from the ground into a gully as it begins its journey south. The other spring is contained in a quiet pond, some 200 years old. Steep valleys and ravines take the water to the series of five lakes which were once the feeder ponds for the furnaces further downstream. School parties make occasional visits to the park for a guided tour of the source streams, for the Cuckmere river is part of the school curriculum.

It is June 1957 and the 2.39pm train from Tunbridge Wells to Eastbourne steams through the tunnel and past the natural gas container on its way through Heathfield to Eastbourne. *Photo by Peter Hay.*

The Cuckoo Line

The Waldron Ghyll, another source stream of the Cuckmere, rises in modern Heathfield, the town which grew up round the station built in 1881 as part of the single track Tunbridge Wells to Eastbourne railway. Railway workers nicknamed the track the Cuckoo Line after the Sussex tradition that the first cuckoo of spring was released at Heathfield fair. For more than 80 years its trains served the country areas, and a small electric tramway extended from the station at Hellingly to what was then called the Mental Asylum. There were many steep gradients and curves on the line and the drivers of the steam-powered engines were sternly warned: 'Time must not be made up in running down inclines'. One driver had already tried this once too often, between Heathfield and Mayfield, and had been killed when the train came off the rails.

The railway line was well used until the 1960s when it was axed by Dr Beeching, the last passenger train running from Eastbourne to Hailsham on September 9, 1968.

In 1981 East Sussex County Council and Wealden District Council bought the line south of Heathfield for a public trail, but over the next ten years it received little attention and became overgrown. Then, in 1990 the line was given a new lease of life. Wealden formed a partnership with Sustrans, a charity specialising in creating paths for cyclists and walkers, and the first part of the Cuckoo Trail was opened at Heathfield in July 1992, with the Hailsham to Polegate stretch following in September.

The Cuckoo Trail

Access to the trail in Heathfield is indicated by a sign by the former station, now a shop, in Station Road. The route crosses the Ghyll at Horam and follows the line of the easterly streams above Hellingly and the paths and walks around the whole area of the trail cross and recross the Cuckmere's header streams at various points.

Users of the trail will see original sculptures placed as mile posts along the way. Currently there are six, but they have been so much admired that more are to be commissioned. And along the way are carved oak benches, made from oaks felled in the 1987 hurricane.

The Cuckoo Trail today winds through eleven miles of beautiful rolling Sussex countryside, lined with hedges, trees and wild flowers. Since it opened it has proved so popular with walkers, cyclists and riders of all ages that it now forms the spine of a whole series of routes linking towns throughout East Sussex. Eventually, there will be a 2,000 mile network of paths across Britain to commemorate the Millennium.

Cross in Hand. The left fork is the road to Blackboys.

ALONG THE RIDGEWAY AND DOWN THE SLOPES

Leaving Heathfield the A265 curves and straightens to arrive at Cross in Hand and Blackboys, close neighbours on the Wealden ridge. They are only two miles apart and each has an old established inn and a long and varied history. The Darn Stream rises in Heatherden Wood, south of the main road near Cross in Hand, and flows through the gardens of the nearby Leopards Mill with its old pond bay. In 1659 ironmaster John Fuller purchased land in the area, which included fifty acres called 'Leopards', and further downstream is the site of his Waldron furnace.

Cross in Hand

The name Cross in Hand derives, so tradition has it, from the Crusader knights who, each with a cross in his hand, assembled there with their men-at-arms, on their way to the coast to take ship to the Holy Land.

There were two windmills in the village at one time, ideally placed on the high ridge to catch the prevailing winds. The round house of the old mill can still be seen and the new mill, erected in 1855, stands a short distance north of the main road.

Between Cross in Hand and Blackboys the road passes above Selwyns Wood where the Summersbrook rises, and then Possingworth Park, a well-wooded estate with two lakes, where the western source of the Cuckmere begins its journey south. There are two versions of why Blackboys is so called. The first, and most likely, is that it is named after a fifteenth century lord of the manor, Sir Richard Blakeboyes; the second that 'black boys' was the name given to the charcoal burners who worked in the woods and came to the inn to quench their thirst without first washing the soot from their faces.

Waldron

A turning to the south leads to the village of Waldron, listed in the Domesday Book as Waldere and Waldrene. It was later the home of Sir William de Waldrene, Lord Mayor of London in 1412. The oxen that in winter used to pull the carriages of the gentry and the carts and waggons of the farmers through the axle deep mud of the unmade roads of the

Waldron church.

29

Chiddingly church with its 128ft high spire.

Sussex countryside gave Oxpasture Wood its name. They would no doubt have been used on occasions for the funerals of members of the Fuller family who were laid to rest in the churchyard. There were so many of them that one vicar suggested calling the area occupied by their graves 'Fullers Earth'.

Chiddingly

From Waldron follow the road south, where the Darn and the Summersbrook drop down more than 400 feet to meet two more source streams of the Cuckmere at Chiddingly. This village has an inn called the Six Bells, a shop and an imposing church with a 128ft high stone spire. Until recently the name of the inn agreed with the number of bells in the church tower but in 1998 , as a millennium project, two additional bells were added and now the bellringers can do thousands rather than just hundreds of changes. Inside the church is the recently restored Jefferay Monument of 1612. It stands against the south transept walls and has an alabaster effigy of Sir John Jefferay in his robes as Lord Chief Baron of the Exchequer under Queen Elizabeth I. With him is his wife Alice, and their daughter Elizabeth, and her husband, Sir Edward Montague.

The Jefferays, it was said, were so proud that they did not like their feet to touch the ground – so cheeses were placed for them to use as stepping stones on their way to the church. The round plinths on which Sir John's daughter and son-in-law stand supposedly represent these cheeses.

Pictured right is a postcard of the monument, dating from the 1900s when the postage on it was a halfpenny. It is an early example of a mistake that is still being made, for printed in red above the picture is: 'Judge Jeffery Monument, Chiddingly Church, Sussex', which gives the impression that the wicked Judge Jefferys of the 'Bloody Assizes' is the subject of the memorial rather than that upright statesman, Sir John Jefferay.

The Onion Pie Murder

In 1851 Stream Farm, Chiddingly was the scene of what became known as the Onion Pie Murder. When William French, a 35 year old labourer came home from work on Christmas Eve he found his wife, Sarah, with their 20 year old lodger, James Hickman, who was supposedly courting Sarah's sister. William was none too pleased to find the two together but he said nothing and settled down to his dinner of a fine onion pie.

Later he complained of feeling ill and for two days he was unable to go to work but returned on the third day, telling a friend that the onion pie must have 'interrupted his insides'. A few days later William French was dead.

The jury at the inquest at the Gun Inn found French's death was due to natural causes but rumours of Sarah's involvement with Hickman began to circulate and soon reached the ears of the police. Sarah French was taken into custody while her husband's body was exhumed and, after a second inquest, she was charged with his murder.

The case, when it came to trial, was known as the Onion Pie Murder. Both Hickman and Sarah gave conflicting accounts of who had added arsenic to the onion pie William French had eaten with such relish. Judge and jury accepted Hickman's version of what had occurred and Sarah was found guilty of wilful murder and hanged before a crowd of 4,000 in Lewes on 10 April 1852.

Before her execution Sarah French made a statement exonerating Hickman and admitted giving the arsenic to her husband. Perhaps this last minute confession was her way of saving her former lover from continuing suspicion in respect of the dreadful deed. In spite of the jury's obvious misgivings the police did not pursue the matter. Few in the crowd at one of the last public executions in Lewes knew that Sarah and William French's small son, a boy of seven, had been put into the workhouse to be cared for. Later he was taken to live with a relative in the hope that, with the resilience of childhood, he would grow up to lead a life unscarred by the tragedy.

5

TO THE WEST

On the southern side of the A22 between East Hoathly and the Boship roundabout are the villages of Lower Dicker and Upper Dicker. This being Sussex, Upper Dicker is below Lower Dicker. For centuries the Dicker was common land but later there were disputes about the ownership of such places as Cromerlotte, now known as Camberlot and Bowershipp, now Boship. They were finally settled in 1870 and it was formally recorded that: 'Dicker is a common now enclosed'.

  Near Golden Cross a tributary of the Cuckmere, the Wick Street stream, winds round Deanland Wood. In the 1950s this wood was home to a thriving nudist colony but no longer. The southern end is now used as a park for modern mobile homes.

Deanland airfield in war and peace

During the Second World War the open land across the lane that bounds the wood on the west was an airfield. It was built in 1943 as a fighter base and used also as an emergency landing ground for aircraft damaged or running low on fuel. It was a grass airfield with two Summerfield track runways of wire mesh. The length of the main runway was 4,800 feet, the second, 4,200 feet, there were four hangars and four hard standings for aircraft refuelling. Broadacres, Broomham Farm and Cleggetts Farm were requisitioned for use as officers' quarters, offices, an armoury and a mess and Nissen huts provided additional accommodation.

  By August 1943 the first runway was completed and Deanland became immediately operational as an emergency landing ground. First to land there was a wounded Spitfire pilot followed on 6 September by a B17 Flying Fortress returning from a bombing mission to Stuttgart and desperately short of fuel. At dusk on 16 September some nineteen Flying Fortresses, some damaged and all short of fuel, landed one after the other. Three crashed on landing but nearly all the others were able to fly out again after refuelling. The base was officially opened on 1 April 1944 with the arrival of three Polish squadrons formed from airmen from that country who had escaped after the German invasion. They trained on Mark IX Spitfires and went on sorties over France as escorts and on deep penetration flights.

The Poles did not stay long at Deanland, moving on to bases at Chailey, Ford, and then across to France in August of that year. Three more squadrons of Spitfires arrived, their role to provide escorts for the bombers softening up the Atlantic Wall defences. The invasion of Normandy on 6 June saw the planes from Deanland used at full stretch over the beachheads. No 611 squadron was airborne at 3am and was the first British fighter squadron over the invasion beaches of Gold and Omaha. Two other squadrons escorted tugs and gliders to Normandy and carried out missions against German positions.

Deanland airfield today is still used by private fliers. Pictured is a French Emerald monoplane ready for take-off.

June of that fateful year saw the flying bombs, the V1s, droning over the southern skies, their pulse jets making the distinctive sound that immediately earned them the name of 'Doodlebugs'. Fighter planes of 91 and 322 squadrons moved to Deanland in July to intercept the new menace, achieving 293 'kills' between them. Flying Officer Ken Collier of 91 Squadron was the first to use the technique of tipping over a V1 with the wings of his Spitfire and causing it to crash.

During its short life as a wartime airfield – it was last used in October 1944 and then officially closed – Deanland saw triumph and tragedy. Inevitably some pilots were killed in their battle with the Doodlebugs but twenty two of those based there achieved four or more 'kills' each, saving many other lives in the process. After the war the airfield site reverted to agricultural use but in the 1960s the land was bought by Richard Chandless who had obtained a pilot's licence. With the aid of friends interested in flying he laid out a landing strip on the site of the southern end of one of the two war-time runways and constructed a small hangar. In 1992 Deanland had new owners; two main hangars; around ten aeroplanes based there; and was certificated for use as a private airfield.

On 4-6 June 1994 the fiftieth anniversary of the D-Day landings were commemorated throughout the country. Deanland Wood Park staged a flying display by a Spitfire and on the 6 June thirty five visiting aircraft flew in to the airfield. A painting showing the various squadron insignia was unveiled and presented to Ripe Church where it can now be seen.

Famous fraudster moves to The Dicker

After leaving Deanland the Wick Street stream flows east and south to skirt the village known simply as The Dicker. In the large house there that is now St Bedes School once lived a man referred to in biographical dictionaries as 'English journalist and criminal'. Horatio Bottomley was born in 1860 in lowly circumstances. He absconded from an orphanage at the age of fourteen, finding work in London as an errand boy in a solicitor's office. He then became a court shorthand writer and, after marrying in 1880, settled in Clapham. In 1884 Bottomley began his long career in publishing with a weekly newspaper, the *Hackney Hansard*. By 1891 it had to close, leaving him bankrupt. Brought to court for fraud, the silver tongued man defended himself so well that he was acquitted.

Horatio Botttomley's house – now St Bede's School – at Lower Dicker.

Completely undeterred by this setback Bottomley plunged headlong into finance, floating companies of more than doubtful validity. In spite of sixty seven bankruptcy petitions against him in the course of four years he managed to amass a fortune of several million pounds and in 1898 became editor of the *Financial Times*. However, the newspaper with which his name is always associated is *John Bull* which he founded in 1906. Edited by Bottomley, it was a sensational success, both loved for its defence of private rights and feared for its exposure of what it claimed to be public wrongs.

Meanwhile the money continued to flow in and just as quickly out again. The free spending Bottomley built a mansion at The Dicker to serve as his country retreat and in his happy new guise as a country squire did very well with his stable of racehorses, some of which were trained at the Winton stables at Alfriston. There, in one of his usual bursts of generosity, he built a house for his trainer on the banks of the Cuckmere river. The prize money from his racing successes helped to finance a continuous round of gaiety – mistresses in London, much entertaining and showering his friends with gifts. The people of the

Dickers unreservedly loved this soldier of fortune. He was president of the Dicker Cricket Club and also the owner of the only telephone in the village, which he allowed everyone to use.

Bottomley served as an independent MP for South Hackney from 1906-12 and, helped by his patriotic speeches and his editorials in *John Bull*, was re-elected in 1918. His downfall came in 1922 when his crafty scheme for attracting investment in government War Bonds and diverting it to his own use came unstuck. He was found guilty of fraud on twenty three counts out of twenty four and was sentenced to seven years in prison.

Released in 1927, Bottomley returned to his home at The Dicker and a warm welcome from the local people, who loved him still. Banners and bunting and the Hailsham Prize Band added to the country-wide celebration of his freedom. But the end of the greatest con-man of the century was a sad one. The failure of his new weekly, *John Blunt*, in 1928 and the death of his always loyal wife in 1930, destroyed his spirit. Horatio Bottomley died in 1933, a poor man. His ashes were scattered on the Downs above Alfriston where the horses that he loved had every morning been exercised on the gallops.

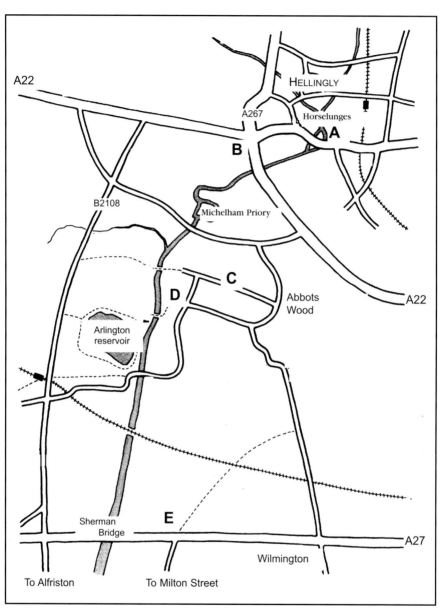

Sketch map of the lower reaches from Hellingly to Sherman Bridge on the A27.
A: Horsebridge watermill, B: Boship Hotel, C: Bates Green (start of Bluebell
Walk), D: Arlington church, E: Site of Wilmington airfield.

38

6

TURNING EAST

The hamlets which form part of the parish of Chiddingly are scattered and linked by narrow tree-lined lanes which pass over small stone bridges spanning the Cuckmere streams. Hamly Bridge crosses the Bull River and the lane leads east past Gun Hill and joins the A267. A mile or two further to the north is Horam. Its name comes from the Saxon *Horham*, literally meaning 'a dirty settlement'. Possibly the Cuckmere streams were to blame for this unflattering name by making the site muddy when they overflowed after heavy rains. They are better behaved today and although they run close to the village they do not flood into it.

When the Wealden iron industry was at its height Horam was a major centre with eight blast furnaces and five power forges. These, together with the seven more primitive bloomery workings, all lay within a four mile radius of the village. The iron workings which flourished in the High Weald were totally unlike the iron mills of the north and Midlands where the chimneys belched thick dark smoke from coal furnaces, truly earning the area the title of 'Black Country'. The tree felling which caused concern at the time was on the whole well managed and replaced by generous planting and the old hammer ponds that remain have enhanced the natural surroundings.

Old Horam Manor
One of these legacies of the past is evident at Old Horam Manor which stands on the southern outskirts of Horam. The entrance to the grounds is from the A267 to the right of Horam village hall and there are camping facilities and a nature trail that leads through woodland past a series of

Horam Manor as it was in the eighteenth century and, below, one of the string of ponds leading down to the Darn Stream.

large ponds. The house itself faces south and part of it dates back to the fifteenth century. Here the visitor can see the old weathered farmyard buildings, barns and stables, for this is a working farm of some acreage and the woods and ponds attract a large number of birds, including woodpeckers, heron and kingfisher.

In this rural setting are strong echoes of the area's industrial past in its series of ponds and the discovery of both iron ore and charcoal on the estate, once the property of the Dyke family which had interests in the iron workings of Sussex, Kent and Yorkshire. In the tea room, housed in a great barn, is an exhibition charting the history of the iron industry in Sussex from Roman times. It includes examples of iron ore, an enormous pair of bellows, and a section of railings forged from Sussex iron which were made for St Paul's Cathedral and dismantled in 1911.

Sir Christopher Wren's accounts, which are preserved at St Paul's cathedral, give details of the cost of the 'large iron ffence round the church' in 1714. The total weight of the 'rails, bolts, balasters, scrowles, rails, spikes and stubs and braces' was just over 207 tons and the total cost of the iron was £11,202 0s 6d. Patterns for the rails cost £50 and the charge for putting up the gates was a further £50.

The owner of Horam Manor Farm is keen to establish an historic ironworking centre there with a reconstruction of all the processes from ore mining, the old type of bloomery workings, coppicing and charcoal burning, together with a forge and furnace complex with exact reconstructions of the buildings and methods used. Meanwhile the farm complex, camp site and nature trail are open to visitors from late spring through to the autumn. The ponds leading down to the Darn Stream were used at one time for breeding carp and now they are a favourite haunt of anglers in the coarse fishing season.

The making of Merrydown

The original Horam Manor, built by Sir Thomas Dyke, was an imposing Jacobean mansion. Like many country estates its fortunes changed over the centuries and by the the 1930s it was a country house hotel. A serious fire in 1941 left the building derelict – and so it remained until 1947 when it was bought for £3,500 by Ian Howie as a new base for what was to become a successful wine and cider making business.

The story of the Merrydown Wine company and its founding partners owes much to the long arm of fate. Three small boys living in

The Merrydown founders in 1954. L to r John Kellond-Knight, Ian Howie and Jack Ward in front of recently erected 20,000 gallon oak vats.

Eastbourne attended a kindergarten school in Enys Road. Jack Ward was four years older than Ian Howie and John Kellond-Knight but the families lived close by and were friendly with each other. Many years later, after the Second World War, the childhood association was to be renewed by grown men who had pursued different careers but who eventually came together to establish one of the most enterprising businesses in Sussex.

Jack Ward had married early in 1939 and he and his new wife bought a house called Merrydown near Rotherfield and here after the war Jack and Ian Howie decided to take the plunge and start their own wine making business. John Kellond-Knight, now married with a young son, joined them, with his small family housed in a caravan nearby. The three men each put £100 into the business; a 300 year old wooden cider press was borrowed from a friendly farmer; and the first pressing of vintage cider took place. These were young men's dreams and needed young men's energies to find carboys, sugar, bottles, cleaning equipment, and most of all perhaps, optimism and an irrepressible sense of humour. Their early travels and war experiences had prepared them well for all the pitfalls of setting up an untried business and with the purchase of an old Nissen hut and the discovery of wine yeast that could be sent from Switzerland they managed to keep going, with the partners taking other jobs to keep the money coming in.

Ian Howie decided to buy the derelict Horam Manor with inherited money at about the time that the then Chancellor of the Exhequer, Sir Stafford Cripps, decided to double the duty on French wine. Vintage cider, although of equal strength to wine, became duty free. By 1985 Merrydown's profits reached the £1m mark for the first time – a giant step from beginnings with a small cider press in a garage.

John Kellond-Knight had left in 1956 to live in Australia but Ian Howie and Jack Ward stayed on to steer the firm through the changes of methods and production which for a time included the firm's own vineyard at Horam. Both men died in 1986. Ian Howie went out in style, quickly and suddenly, when he suffered a heart attack soon after a lunch at the Savoy Hotel in London at the expense of the bank. Jack Ward followed his old friend in August of the same year.

Vines Cross

Past the Merrydown premises the road through Horam dips sharply downhill and a turning to the right leads over Horeham Bridge to Vines Cross. The Cuckmere source streams follow courses east and west of the village and one of the bridges that spanned them collapsed under the weight of an early traction engine. It is commemorated by the inn sign of the Brewer's Arms which pictures the river with its wooden bridge and the local name of the inn – the Clappers. Many footpaths cross the fields in this area and the bar of the Clappers is a good place to make for after a walk. It has a friendly atmosphere,

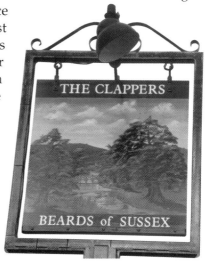

a collection of old bicycles hanging from the ceiling and books and pictures on its wood panelled walls. A short distance north of Vines Cross Hammer Lane leads across to Warbleton, so completing the full circle of the upper reaches of the Cuckmere streams.

Now it is time to turn south and follow one of the lanes that lead to Hellingly, which has the Bull river to the west and the main waters of the Cuckmere from Waldron Ghyll and the Vines Cross stream to the east. The village was originally an early Saxon settlement or *leah* and the first part of this unusual name comes from the Saxon word *hielle*, which means tongue of land.

The Old Mill House at Hellingly

The water mill in the grounds of Old Mill House on the north west of the village is enclosed by two streams of the Cuckmere. There was a mill on the site at the time of the Domesday survey of 1086 and in 1255 there was a dispute about water rights between the Abbot of Battle and Prior Peter of Michelham. The case was decided in the abbot's favour by the King's justices sitting at Chichester on 18 November that year and the prior was ordered to pay the abbot, as the owner of the mill, ten shillings a year and maintain a certain water level at the mill head.

In the 1930s the Old Mill House was opened as a private hotel and, according to its brochure, 'the old mill wheel and machinery was used, without any alterations or new additions, to provide the power for generating electric light throughout the entire establishment and also in certain parts of the garden.' The brochure goes on to describe the attractions which include 'a delightful private stretch of about one mile of the River Cuckmere flowing through the grounds which affords safe boating; a tennis court, golf course and a billiards table. Lunch, tea, supper or light refreshments may be obtained at any time, either served in the Old Mill, or on the tea lawn overlooking the trout pool and waterfall'.

The present brick and timber framed mill was built in the eighteenth century and was in use as a corn mill until 1922. After it ceased to be a working mill the buildings became derelict but in 1938 a new owner restored the machinery and turned the premises into the Old Water Mill Tea Rooms.

A famous playwright and the Press

In the 1960s the property was bought as a country retreat by John Osborne, the controversial and outspoken actor turned playwright whose *Look Back in Anger,* first produced in 1956, introduced 'angry young men' to the British theatre. Osborne went on to write many other successful plays, including *The Entertainer,* and also had a varied and stormy love life which made him an object of great interest to the news media. Consequently when he arrived at his new home, having slipped quietly away from London with Penelope Gilliatt, the journalist and author, he was more than a little dismayed to find the narrow lane full of cars and to be greeted with a battery of flashbulbs and shouted questions. The reporters were not only in his drive but in the house too, a friend having invited them inside, and something very like a party had developed while they were awaiting their prey. After an hour everyone departed in good spirits and a Sunday paper front-paged the story with the headline: 'JOHN OSBORNE AND FRIEND IN MYSTERY MIDNIGHT MOVE'.

The twelfth century church of St Peter and St Paul in Mill Lane, Hellingly.

Despite the disclosure of the location of his country retreat John Osborne stayed for some years time at the old water mill and wrote yet another successful play, Inadmissable Evidence, while he was there. On 25 May, 1963, at Hailsham Registry Office, Penelope Gilliatt became his third wife, an occasion again well attended by the press. In the 1970s more restoration work was done at the mill by its new owner, Jonathan Minns, the founder and director of the British Engineerium at Hove, as a result of which it is now preserved as a typical Sussex rural mill.

From Hellingly, with its picturesque old houses clustered round the church, there is access to the Cuckoo Trail and Church Lane runs close to the tree-lined banks of the Bull river.

South of the main road is the entrance to Horselunges Manor, a fifteenth century timber framed building built on a much older moated site. Its odd name may well be a corruption of the names of two early owners, the Hersts and the Lyngyvers. It was while poaching near Horselunges in 1541 that Lord Dacre of Herstmonceux murdered a gamekeeper and was hanged at Tyburn for his crime. And it is next to the manor house that the Cuckmere's two main streams from the north finally come together to continue their journey across the Vale of Sussex.

7

AT LAST – ONE RIVER

One river, one name at last, the source streams have converged from their many winding courses. Although the distance from the Heathfield ridge to Hellingly is but nine miles as the crow flies, it is almost the halfway mark on its journey to the sea. Further south the valley widens as it follows the contour at the foot of the hills through the gap in the South Downs. Ten thousand years ago, as the thaw began after the last Ice Age, the Cuckmere ran through a much deeper valley, continuing south to join the great Seine/Solent river system. This great river flowed west through what were then the lowlands between Britain and the continent of Europe, to meet an Atlantic coast which stretched between Brittany and Cornwall.

The rise in sea level caused by the melting ice, a process which continues to this day, gave birth to the English Channel and a closer union with the rivers and the sea. The southern end of the Cuckmere valley was an estuary in past centuries and in Roman times the cliffs on each side of the haven extended at least a mile further out to sea than they do today. This area was a salt marsh 500 years ago as a result of a minor rise in sea level and below the surface of the valley floor lie many metres of alluvial silt. It is thought that below this there could be up to 10 metres of peat, formed from decaying alder swamp vegetation which grew here between about 4000 and 1200 BC

Floods in the flood plain

Today a well defined flood plain extends from the mouth of the river at Cuckmere Haven inland to Hellingly, its width varying from 500 metres in the tidal reaches up to Milton Lock, which stands a little north of Alfriston, and 50 metres in the upper reaches. The gentle Cuckmere often seems little more than a stream as it flows through its narrow banks but it can change quickly when heavy rains and high tides unleash its power. The valley has been flooded many times in the past but with the cut made in 1846 from Exceat Bridge to bypass the meanders which curve across the last mile to the mouth, the river was given a more direct access to the sea. Nowadays, in extreme weather conditions, flood warnings are given to those areas at risk.

In 1974 houses at Alfriston and two cottages near the church at Hellingly were flooded when the river overflowed its banks, as were the water meadows and roads adjoining the river. Older people in this locality remember that as children they saw the river rise to the level of the Grove Bridge at Hellingly. Today the Environment Agency uses control structures, which include weirs at Arlington, Sessingham and Michelham Priory, gauges at Cowbeech, the Lea and Sherman bridges, and sluice gates at Horsebridge and Hellingly, to keep the waters in check. The gates of Milton Lock, just north of Alfriston, can be raised to increase the flow through to the sea.

Arlington reservoir

During the excavations for the reservoir at Arlington, pictured below, which was completed in 1971, the tusk of a mammoth, the horn of a bison and the skull of a woolly rhinoceros were unearthed. These creatures

would have roamed southern England 25,000 years ago when it was still in the grip of the Ice Age. The reservoir. which is within a former loop of the Cuckmere river, covers 49 hectares, equal to the size of 121 football pitches. The shoreline is 2.8km in length and footpaths wind around the lake and through the wooded area on the northern shores.

Although constructed for practical purposes to ensure water supplies for neighbouring towns and villages, the land surrounding the reservoir has become a valued nature reserve. A fishing club has been established and in addition to coarse fish the waters are stocked with trout. Birds love the place and 10,000 wildfowl spend the winter at the lake, with mallard, widgeon and shoveler duck, Canada Geese, tufted duck and pochard among the visitors. Of the 173 bird species recorded there, more unusual waders are seen from July to September. It is also a favourite spot for the passing traffic of spring and autumn migrations. Ospreys have been occasional callers and a nesting platform has been constructed in the hope that one day they might view the lake and neighbouring forest with favour and decide to stay.

The river does not flow directly into the reservoir but its waters can be pumped in when necessary and in drought conditions waters from the River Ouse can be piped to the Arlington treatment works. Just below the pumping station buildings on the eastern banks the lane crosses the river at Chilver Bridge. Here there was once a ford, one used perhaps by the Roman legions on the march along Farnestreet east to the fort at Pevensey, which they named Anderida.

Milton lock and the tidal river

The automated gates at Milton Lock at the head of the tidal waters also serve to keep the river water above the lock clear of salt so it can be used to irrigate farmland. Berwick Court Farm lies close to the river just above the lock and there have been at least three water mills on this site. Before the lock was built and the river embanked, in times of heavy rains and long tides the width of the valley between the hills was often completely covered by water. The great storm of 1703 caused havoc all along the southern coast and on the Cuckmere the miller at Berwick and his men were unable to save the water mill from damage as they were 'so washed by the sea, beating against them like the breaking of waves' although three miles from the river's mouth. This was an exceptional

Top of a spring tide near Milton lock.

storm, the one responsible for much of the destruction of the great beach and part of the fishing village of Brighton, then called Brighthelmstone. The rise and fall of the tides are noticeable from Alfriston down to the sea. During autumn and winter storms the river fills to the top of the embanked sides and spreads its flood across the nearby fields, a reminder that in the past the Cuckmere was wider than it is today, with narrow creeks reaching into the clefts of the hills.

River traffic

Boats have used the lower stretches since early times and possibly the Caen stone shipped from Normandy for the building of both Wilmington and Michelham priories may have arrived via the river. Later the shingle bank that had built up at the mouth put a stop to river traffic for many years but it was eventually cleared and access from the sea established again.

Below Milton Lock the stone arch of Longbridge crosses the Cuckmere and by the eighteenth century coal, sand for building works, seaweed for fertilising the land and other goods were being brought up river to this point by shallow draught sailing barges. John Lower, born in 1735, was the first man to revive the river traffic and in 1801, the year of his death, two boats were still listed as trading on the Cuckmere as far as Alfriston. Carrying on the family tradition, *The Adventurer* had Charles Lower as its master, although owned by William Stevens of Berwick, and *The Goodwill* was owned by Sarah Lower, with Thomas Lower as master. The old wharf at the end of River Lane in Alfriston close to the Plonk Bridge, sometimes called the White Bridge, saw the last voyage of a commercial barge, *Iona* in 1915. Her master, 'Captain' Nye is buried in St Andrew's churchyard.

In the natural order of things the flow of fresh water is a precious commodity and the river has always been home to a wonderful variety of fish, birds, and animal life. Thriving families of swans know the lower reaches well and all of its tributaries and streams. The birds mate for life and they build their nests on the banks and can often be seen flying down the valley, their wide wings beating a strong rhythm in the air. Reeds and rushes in the marshy areas are home to the warblers and the river banks give haven to water rats and the auburn-coated stoat.

An unconcerned otter

Near the steep curve of river below Hindover hill a few years ago I stopped on a walk up the banks to Alfriston to eat sandwiches and rest. Lazing on the warm turf a sound of splashing made me turn round to see what was happening. An otter appeared. Not only did he seem unconcerned by a human watching him but came gleaming out of the water to have a good look. Completely unafraid, he stared with bright black eyes and twitching whiskers until apparently having satisfied his curiosity, he slid back into the water and splashed on his way downstream. Perhaps he was young, perhaps he had lost the fear of man; a hopeful sign, because otters used to be cruelly hunted. I continued on the path upstream, utterly enchanted by such a rare sight. Some fisherman near the bridge at Alfriston told me that they, too, had seen otters playing in the river near the bend near the church. Otters have also been seen near Arlington in recent years so it seems likely that with continued careful monitoring of the agrichemicals which once polluted the rivers, these elusive and cautious creatures are once more establishing a small and growing population on the Cuckmere.

51

The Cuckmere meanders and the cut.

The last mile of the river's course takes two paths, one through the man-made cut to the river mouth and the other by the widely curving meanders which almost cross the valley floor. In season Canada Geese feed on the grass here in their hundreds and the heron stands thin and still on the river bank waiting for an unwary fish to pass. As the tide goes out mud flats are exposed and the feet of wading birds make criss cross patterns as they feed on the gleaming surface. The meanders end in a man-made lagoon which has become naturalised and provides another haven for birds.

The waters here find their way to the sea through the shingle beach, a broad ridge which stretches across the width of the valley between the cliffs. This ridge is a natural result of longshore drift and winter storms and gives protection from the sea to the land behind the shingle although the drifting pebbles are nowadays carefully monitored to ensure the river's main flow to the sea from the cut is not blocked. Strong retaining groynes of oak have been built at the mouth of the cut and even at low tide the flow here is swift. At high tide the green rush of water swirls past the wooden groyne in strong eddies and currents as at last the river meets the sea.

8

GOING SOUTH

From the halfway point at Hellingly the Cuckmere flows south through fields, briefly dividing into two arms which come together again just below Horsebridge. Close to the main road on the site of an engineering works, is the tall building of an old mill which was rebuilt in 1884 after being burnt out in a fire. Horsebridge Mill took its power from the river passing beneath its 5.2m undershot water wheel and in the early 1800s was grinding between ten and fourteen loads of wheat each week.

The water wheel, right, was built by Upfield of Catsfield and was renovated in 1939 and continued to supply power for another five years until electricity took over. The mill closed in 1969 but the sluice gate is still used to control the flows and prevent flooding.

There are two bridges across the Cuckmere here – Mill Bridge and the Horse Bridge, a little to the west. The river makes its winding way south west and is joined by a stream flowing past Lower Horsebridge. It passes under the busy A22 Eastbourne to London road, almost unnoticed by the fast traffic and flows past the grounds of the

Boship Hotel and under Hempstead Bridge. The hotel, now a popular conference centre and with a restaurant and bar open to non residents, has fishing rights on the north bank of the river.

Hailsham and the hangman's rope

South of Boship the river winds south and west and is joined by a tributary stream called the Knockhatch, which flows from the outskirts of Hailsham. This busy market town was originally the 'ham' or settlement of a Saxon called *Haegel*, and is recorded in the Domesday Book as Hamelsham, with land for four ploughs. By the time of the Tudors the name of the town had changed to Heylsome and some local people still use this form of pronunciation. The fifteenth century church of St Mary's is on the site of a Norman church which was originally the site of a Saxon moot or meeting place.

In pre-Conquest days an old embayment of the sea reached far inland across what are now the reclaimed fields of the Pevensey levels. The sea lapped the shores of Herstmonceux and Hailsham and the extraction of salt from these waters was a profitable and necessary industry as salt was used extensively for the preservation of food. Hailsham had thirteen salthouses or saltpans. The salt was extracted either by evaporation from the heat of the sun on the open pans or by heating the briny water in the salthouses until only the salt remained. The town was granted a market charter in 1252 and by 1834 it had one of the largest cattle and corn markets in Sussex, with drovers bringing their stock from as far away as Wales. There was a barracks, a busy brickfield, and in 1807 Thomas Burfield embarked on his successful business of rope making, a product for which Hailsham became famous.

Until the early 1900s there were eight ropewalks around the town, one of them behind the site of the present day Woolworths in the High Street. Outworkers would tie about 40lbs of hemp round their waists and, attaching an end to the spinning wheel, walk backwards down the walk paying out line and twisting the thread. As more modern methods evolved the industry grew to produce everything from the massive ropes for ships down to the humble clothes line and many other by-products of hemp. In *Cassell's Magazine* of 1898 is the macabre note: 'All the ropes for capital punishment used by the government at home and in the colonies, are made in Hailsham'.

The cattle market has gone now, much to the dismay of local people, but there is a weekly market on the old site on Fridays. The tradition of rope making continues with Marlow Ropes now manufacturing from stronger man-made materials every type of rope needed for to-day's world, including that for maritime use and the strong lines needed for rock climbing.

Today the town is still growing. It has almost joined up with its old neighbours of Hellingly and Horsebridge and has an established and traditional High Street of shops which retain the friendly atmosphere of a true market town. East of Hailsham the river's course heads into the countryside away from the main London road, the narrow stream passing close to the 880 acres of Wilmington Forest.

Arlington Speedway

On the northern edge of the woodland, well signposted from the A22, a road leads to the Arlington Speedway stadium. Here, twice a week on summer evenings, the exciting sound of powerful engines echoes over the trees and the smell of burning oil and rubber brings a whiff of modern life to the outskirts of the ancient forest. The track was built in 1928 and the first meeting took place the following year. Arlington is one of the original tracks on which speedway started and it is now the oldest speedway track still in operation. In 1954 stock car racing became an additional attraction and now, from mid March to the end of October every year, the speedway bikes race on Saturday evenings and stock cars on Wednesdays. There are thrills and spills aplenty. The speedway riders, wearing highly coloured leathers, are astride 500cc machines on a circuit of 300 metres. These high powered motorcycles reach speeds of more than 70mph on the straights and the riders turn sharply into the bends without the aid of gears or brakes. The resident Eastbourne Eagles speedway team are professionals, the riders racing in Britain for eight months of the year and abroad during the winter season.

The team competes in the British League First Division and has an impressive reputation, having won the National League title on four occasions and the Knockout Cup six times in the last 20 years. The club has produced a number of World Finalists and fans come from far and wide to the meetings, spectators averaging 2,000 for each event, with television coverage two or three times a year.

The lake in Abbots Wood.

In the quiet reaches of the forest, which was once part of the old Saxon *Andredsweald* which stretched across south east England from Kent to Hampshire, a quarter of the woodland is of the broad-leaved variety of trees. The Forestry Commission, which now owns and conserves the land, has planted conifers too, and these are thinned and felled for commercial purposes. The forest has provided firewood and timber for the nearby villages and towns for centuries and records show that the woods were cleared three times in the sixteenth century. Young trees always grew to take their place and although a great part of the forest was cleared again during the Second World War for much needed timber, the woodlands are now carefully managed and almost restored to their former glory.

In spring the ground under the broad-leaved trees is covered with a mass of anemones and bluebells and, as it is warm here in the summer months, the open clearings have many wild flowers and grasses which attract butterflies, dragonflies and a wide variety of birds. Rabbits abound and in the beginning of this century members of the Cacklebury Gang of poachers came softly here on moonlit nights. There are foxes too, and if you come to these woods in the early morning or late evening you may catch sight of the elusive badger.

Walks in Abbots Wood

Wilmington Forest once belonged to Battle Abbey and a part of the forest is still known as Abbots Wood which today is a favoured place for walkers. Following the road from the A22 past the speedway stadium, a left hand fork in the road towards Arlington village will lead to the wood and a large car park. There are seats and picnic tables and well signposted paths into the forest. An information leaflet and map is available detailing the two mile main walk and a 1fi mile variation. The half mile Placket Walk is well surfaced and especially designed for disabled visitors.

The lake, which is passed on the western shore on the main walk, is one of three ponds believed to have been built in the thirteenth century as a source of fish for the abbey and the nearby Michelham Priory. In 1964 the Forestry Commission cleaned and restored the lake which is linked by a stream to the Cuckmere. The fishing rights are leased to Hailsham Angling Association but day tickets are available.

The gatehouse of Michelham Priory and, below, the water mill.

Close to Abbots Wood is Bates Green Farm where, since 1972, the annual Bluebell Walk and Farm Trail has been open every spring. This well organised event is immensely popular. There is car parking in an adjacent field and refreshments available at the farm. The well marked paths wind through beautiful woodland filled with the scent and colour of thousands of bluebells and small signs give information on the trees and the natural habitat. The dates of the Bluebell Walk vary slightly each year but are well advertised locally.

Michelham Priory

A mile from the forest is Michelham Priory in its seven acres of moated grounds. This moat, which is one of the longest in England, was formed by damming the Cuckmere river. In 1229 an Augustinian priory was founded here by Gilbert de Aquila, Lord of Pevensey. The Augustinians, who were known as Black Canons from the colour of their habits, were ordained priests who renounced worldly belongings and lived a disciplined communal life, maintaining a daily round of prayer and with the help of lay brothers running the priory and grounds. They dispensed hospitality to travellers both rich and poor and in September 1302 they entertained the royal household of King Edward 1 who was on yet another progress from Surrey through Sussex to Kent.

After Henry VIII's dissolution of the monasteries in 1536 the priory fell into disrepair. It was sold by the Crown and had two changes of ownership before Herbert Pelham purchased it in 1587 and incorporated what remained of the priory into a fine Tudor house. Pelham's lavish spending brought about his downfall and before the century was out he was declared bankrupt and Michelham was sold to the Sackvilles and remained as part of their extensive estates for nearly 300 years. In 1896 James Gwynne of Folkington Manor bought the priory and began an ambitious programme of renovation. It was sold again in 1924 to Richard Beresford-Wright, parts of the estate being divided into lots and sold at separate sales. The restoration was continued but in 1927 a disastrous fire gutted the Tudor wing, although the original staircase survived.

At the outbreak of the Second World War evacuees from Rotherhithe came to Michelham and the priory later became an Army base for Canadian troops. A plan for the raid of Dieppe in 1942 was drawn on a wall in the gatehouse and can still be seen there today. It changed hands once again in 1951 after the death of Richard Beresford-Wright and was purchased in 1958 by Mrs R H (Stella) Hotblack, who with tremendous enthusiasm converted buildings in the barnyard to provide a restaurant, made a car park and opened the house and grounds to the public. Determined to ensure its safe keeping, this redoubtable lady arranged an endowment from Kenneth, Earl of Inchcape, given as a memorial to a school friend killed in the war, and then presented Michelham Priory in trust to the Sussex Archaeological Society in 1959.

The society has continued works of repair and restoration, returning the historic water mill to working order. The beautiful house of mellow sandstone and its grounds are open to the public from March to October each year. The entrance is through the 60ft high gatehouse which dates from the fourteenth century and the rooms open to the public contain much of interest, covering the centuries from relics of the Stone Age up to Victorian times and a glimpse in the kitchen quarters of how people lived before the days of gas and electricity.

The lawns and gardens are a splendid amalgam of medicinal herb garden, fine herbaceous borders, trees, water, and small paths that twist and turn and suddenly reveal sculptures. Close to the house is a museum with displays of old farming implements and Sussex ironware and a huge Tudor barn in which exhibitions are held. There is a restaurant with additional seating outside and in the grounds and beside the lake there are places to picnic. The water mill, which was used for grinding corn, has been carefully preserved. From it the Cuckmere continues its journey south through shady tree lined banks and it is joined by two more tributaries, the Wick Street stream and the Sessingham stream.

Back on the road which runs alongside the forest is the Old Oak Inn, built in 1733 for £231 11s 6d as the village poorhouse. The cost of the bricks, tiles, timber, doors and windows is all listed in some parish accounts which were discovered in the wall of an old cottage at Locks Farm, Halland when it was demolished in 1957. From here a narrow road leads to the village of Arlington with its part Saxon church on a site which was a cemetery during the Roman occupation. Tenants of the Yew Tree Inn at Arlington paid their rent to this church for nearly 100 years for in 1766 William Harmer and his wife, Ann, had granted it a 999 year lease on the premises. It remained in the possession of the parish until

1837 when the executors of the then rector, the Reverend Thomas Scutt, sold it to Hailsham Brewery. It is now a Harvey's house and has a notice on the door requesting customers not to let the cat in.

Old and new Berwick

Berwick seems to cover a large area for the station and the nearby Berwick Inn are at some distance from the church of St Michael and All Angels and the old village to the south of the main A27 road where there is another inn, the Cricketers Arms.

Berwick is recorded in the Domesday book as Berewice, from the Saxon name, *bere wic*, or barley farm and the church of St Michael and All Angels has stood on the same site for more than 1,000 years. It has had its share of troubles, particularly in the twentieth century. During the Second World War, many of its windows were destroyed by bomb blast. Bishop Bell, Bishop of Chichester from 1929 to 1957, was inspired to have the old leaded windows replaced with plain glass. Now they throw their light on the murals commissioned by Bishop Bell from the Bloomsbury Group artists Duncan Grant, Vanessa Bell and Quentin

The Nativity by Vanessa Bell in St Michael and All Angels.
Photo: D Ellwood

Bell, who were then living at Charleston Farmhouse. *The Nativity* on the north wall of the nave and *The Annunciation* on the south wall are by Vanessa Bell. The *Victor of Calvary* by Duncan Grant is on the west wall and his *Christ in Glory* over the chancel arch. All the paintings in the chancel are by Quentin Bell.

The murals are fully described, as is the history of the church, in a booklet on sale in the nave.

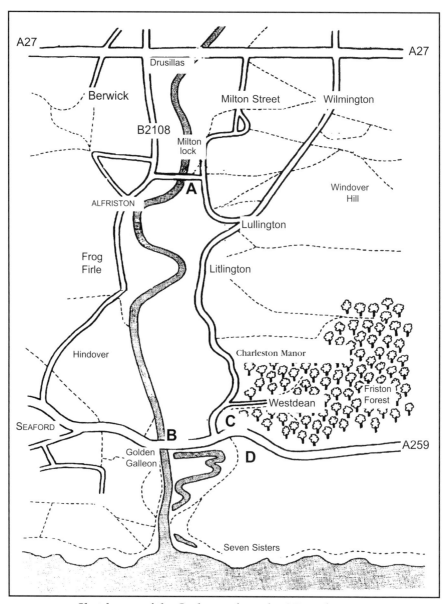

Sketch map of the Cuckmere from the A27 to the coast.
Between A: Long Bridge and B: Exceat Bridge there are footpaths on either side
of the river. C: Country Park Visitors Centre. D: Site of Excete village

9

LAST MILES TO THE SEA

The river now begins the last miles of its journey to the sea, passing under Sherman bridge on the A27 Lewes to Eastbourne road. This bridge gets its name from Shermans Land farm which was there when the road was turnpiked in the eighteenth century. In the fields that lie south of the road, not far from this bridge, is the site of Wilmington airfield. It was used in the First World War as a Home Defence landing ground and was reopened in 1932 as a base for the newly formed Sussex Aviation and Aero Club. A flying circus arrived to give displays and Sir Alan Cobham declared it a perfect place for Eastbourne's Municipal Airport – a pipe dream that came to nothing. Wilmington airfield grew to include a clubhouse, main hangar, and a grass landing area of 400 by 350 yards. De Haviland 60G Moths were used for training and in 1934 Sir Alan returned with his Astra air show. By the end of 1935 a pair of entrepreneurs, T G Stubbley and H A Love, the latter a former First World War pilot with a house directly opposite the airfield, purchased the rights from the original owner and began giving flying lessons under the new name of the Eastbourne Flying Club.

In the mid 1930s flying was all the rage and air shows and pleasure flights were immensely popular. Minister of Transport, Leslie Hore-Belisha, who gave his name to Belisha Beacons, learned to fly there, and also became president of the club. Pioneer airwoman Amy Johnson, the first person to fly solo from London to Australia, visited the airfield and the redoubtable Duchess of Bedford flew her Tiger Moth to many of the air rallies that became a feature at Wilmington.

A *Concours d'Elegance* as part of the flying club's At Home day in August 1936 was such a success the event was repeated the following year, with seventy two visiting aircraft flying in, among them some from Germany . . .

By 1938 a permanent clubhouse had been built and its opening coincided with the annual air show which attracted 10,000 spectators and 100 visiting aircraft. The packed programme included an exhibition of precision flying by the Gloster Gauntlets of No 79 Squadron from Biggin Hill and a display of aerobatics by German air ace, Vera Von Bissing, in her Messerschmitt M35. The last air show, in August 1939, was held under the shadow of the threat of war with Germany but went ahead with its usual international participants. Amazingly there was no hint of nationalistic feeling – until a section of a machine-gun battalion gave a Bren gun display and could not resist the temptation at one stage of pointing their guns at the visiting German aircraft.

When war was declared on 3 September 1939, the club secretary closed the pavilion and hangars for the last time. The keys were handed to an official of the Ministry of Supply but the airfield was not used during the war and was returned to agricultural use. Unlike Deanland, further up the Cuckmere valley, this airfield was never reborn. In 1987 the Tiger Club wished to rebuild the airfield but local people objected and after many heated public meetings and protests the plan was turned down. Today all that is left of this once thriving and historic small aerodrome are the lonely remains of the main hangar, now used for storage by a farmer.

Turning south from the crossroads east of Sherman bridge the road passes through the village of Wilmington and past the twelfth century church which has a huge yew tree in its churchyard. It is believed to be about 1,000 years old and has a girth of 23 feet. At the crest of the road as it leaves Wilmington the north face of Windover Hill comes into view, and with it the Long Man, a 230ft high figure cut into the downland turf. Who he represents, who carved him and what are the rods he has in each hand are questions that have been debated by academics and folklorists over the centuries. Theories about his Neolithic origins were bolstered by the discovery of a Stone Age burial ground on the heights above the figure. Close by are the sites of ancient flint mines and also a Bronze Age burial ground. It is also suggested that the figure is of much later date, perhaps an eighteenth century adornment of the landscape commissioned by a local landowner with antiquarian interests.

The Bluebell Walk in full bloom at Bates Green.

The Bull River at Hellingly and, below, the gatehouse of
Michelham Priory.

Looking towards Exceat from the Golden Galleon.

Water, water everywhere. . . in the last week of 1999 floodwater extended right
across the valley above Exceat.

Swans on the cut by the Golden Galleon at Exceat.

Nobody is sure. What is certain is that the chalk outline of the figure was becoming overgrown by the downland turf and in 1873 it was outlined with yellow bricks. These bricks were replaced in 1969 by white blocks.

The small car park on the right hand side of the road is where a great tithe barn once stood, part of the buildings of the eleventh century Benedictine Priory at Wilmington. It was in this barn that parishioners handed over a tenth part of the annual increase in their 'profits of land, stock on land and their own industry' for the maintenance of their parish priest. In 1836 tithes were replaced by a rent charge but it was not until the Tithe Act of 1936 that this method of maintaining the clergy finally ceased.

Wilmington Priory

Wilmington Priory was founded as a cell of the Abbey of Grestain in Normandy. The French connection caused problems during the series of medieval wars between England and France and the buildings and possessions were confiscated at intervals. The priory was finally seized in 1403 by Henry V and handed over, with the manor, to the diocese of Chichester. After the Dissolution it was given by the Crown to Sir Richard Sackville and from about 1700 the buildings were mainly used as a farm. The beautiful old house is now a private residence.

Beside the road which winds round the lower slopes of Windover hill are two parking places from which there are magnificent views north to the Heathfield ridge and to the west to the curving heights of Firle Beacon. Space, light and colour as far as the eye can see and below the narrow river runs along its tree lined path, passing the quiet lanes of Milton Street where the inn, the Sussex Ox, commemorates the strong patient animals which were used for centuries in farming.

The early days of Drusillas

The old coaching road to Eastbourne used to pass along the top of Windover hill above the Long Man on its way to Jevington and Eastbourne. Across the river are the vineyards of the English Wine Centre, first planted in 1973, just south of the roundabout where the north to south B2108 bisects the west to east A27. A few yards south along the B2108 stands Drusillas, now almost a legend in its own life-time. It was started by Captain Douglas Ann in 1924 as a 'Tea Place' in

Wilmington Priory and, below, the Old Barn Tea Place and Restaurant at
Drusillas in the 1950s

the derelict bone mill, a sixteenth century cottage and some cowsheds that he had bought and restored. From these modest beginnings it has grown over the years into an entertainment complex that includes a zoo, play areas, gardens, restaurants and a train for children.

During the 1930s there were cream teas in the Thatched Barn; supper dances for which tickets were 2s 6d and evening dress was essential, and cinema shows. The zoo had its first chimpanzee and a brown bear, and a steam train took visitors to the banks of the Cuckmere where they could paddle about in punts. Aeroplane flights could be taken in Tiger Moths and Gypsy Moths from an adjoining field – an enterprise run by the owners of the nearby Wilmington Airfield – and there were river trips down to the Golden Galleon at Exceat, which was also owned by Captain Ann.

Everything went so well that 'Tea Room Training' was offered for young gentlewomen wishing to learn cake making and become tea room assistants. For two guineas a week to cover tuition the girls lived at Drusillas and worked from 9am to 7pm. After that their future career was assured. Later, despite the years of war when so many of the bright young things who had danced so happily to the jazzy music of the 1930s had gone, some of them for ever, Drusillas continued to prosper.

In May 1998 it was sold and the name was changed to Drusillas Zoo Park. However the new owners, Laurence and Christine Smith, have three young children – two daughters, Caroline and Cassandra, and a son, Oliver – so once again this popular venue is family owned.

Saxon treasure hoard

South of Drusillas on the road which runs past Berwick House farm to Alfriston, is Winton Street. Here the banks of the narrow lane are high and steep, for this is part of the north-south trackway from the Weald to the coast. Where it meets the east-west track across the Downs is the site of a Saxon burial ground. It was discovered in 1912, when a house was being built, and found to contain 150 graves and a rich hoard of bronze and silver jewellery, of brooches set with garnets and enamel, of crystal necklaces and glass vases, of ornamented buckles and sword pommels, urns and shield bosses. Miss Gregory, for whom the house was being built, put a crucifix on its boundary wall and named it The Sanctuary. Successive owners have not changed the name, nor have they removed the crucifix.

From the viewpoint on Windover hill the lane descends towards Litlington. A pathway on the right hand side of the road leads to Lullington church which stands in a secluded corner overlooking the

valley, and almost hidden by the surrounding trees. It has a local reputation of being the smallest church in England but it is not in the *Guinness Book of Records,* nor is it a complete church but part of the chancel of one dating from the Middle Ages. But what is left there today is pleasingly complete in itself. The tiny church with its white weather boarded belfry can seat twenty people for the services held there once every month and on special occasions, such as the Harvest Festival, room has been found for many more.

Lullington church.

Actor and writer Dirk Bogarde spent happy childhood summers in a cottage nearby and wrote evocatively of this part of the Cuckmere valley in the first volume of his autobiography and in a later book called *Great Meadow.*

The mystery of Burlow Castle

Following the lane downhill towards Litlington a sharp turn to the right past Lullington Court leads back to the Cuckmere and over Long Bridge, a sturdy stone arch with access to footpaths on both banks of the river and a view of Milton Lock a short distance upstream. Not far up river, close to the road which winds down from Milton Street, is the high mound of land called Burlow (or Burlough) Castle. Close to it is a moated site known as The Rookery. Mystery surrounds the origin of these two places. They may have been built long ago as defensive positions and there is no doubt that Burlow Castle, where traces of old stonework still exist, would have been well placed for that purpose in the days when the Viking raiders stormed in from the sea.

Alfriston – the village that has everything

The road over Long Bridge joins the B2108 which leads into the village of Alfriston, named after a Saxon called Aelfric, who was given a farmstead, or tun, here by Alfred the Great as a reward for military service. Alfriston is one of those Sussex villages that is truly all things to all people. It has everything from the small square with the truncated but neat remains of its market cross to a spreading chestnut tree, a real village store and old and beautiful buildings that line the High Street. The Star Inn, with its gaudily painted lion ship's figurehead and timbered and decorative facade, has an equally fascinating interior. Opposite it is the George, an old coaching inn. Every house, every shop, has a history, some of them dating back to the fourteenth century.

There is a Smugglers Inn, once called Market Cross House, where the wicked and daring Stanton Collins lived, and a narrow twitten from the High Street leads to the Tye, where a fete is held every August. The church of St Andrew, known as the Cathedral of the Downs, stands on raised ground on the site of an early monastic church in which the body of St Lewinna, was buried. This young Sussex girl was killed by the

The Smugglers Inn at Alfriston.

73

Alfriston church and in front of it the fourteenth century Clergy House.

The Plonk or White Bridge.

heathen Saxons in the seventh century and her tomb became a place of pilgrimage with a reputation for miracles, until the saint's bones were stolen in 1058 and taken to Flanders.

The church is built in the form of a Greek cross, with materials of local flint, greensand quoins and facings. It is where it is, says a local legend, because God - or the devil - intervened. It was planned for a site near the junction of Weavers Lane and King's Ride and the first foundations were laid there but each morning when the builders arrived, they found their previous day's work undone. Substantial blocks of stone they had carefully put in place were found on the Tye, flung there it seemed by some supernatural agency. It was only when four oxen were found on a mound on the Tye, lying rump to rump in the form of a cross, that the builders got the message – it was the Lord's will that the church should be built where the stones had been thrown and where the oxen now lay.

The path to the left arrives at the Plonk Bridge, which has a notice politely requesting 'riders please dismount'. This wooden bridge is painted white and is sometimes called the White Bridge. Access to the towpaths can be gained from each side of the bridge which is on the South Downs Way. Close to the river on the Tye is the fourteenth century Clergy House, the first historic building to be acquired by the National Trust which bought it for £10 and spent a great deal of money and work on its restoration. Close by is the Wingrove Inn, a colonial style house built in 1870 by the owner of the Wingrove Racing Stables where Longset, the Lincoln winner of 1912 was trained. The adjoining stables and barns have been converted to private houses.

There is a wealth of interest in Alfriston and its surrounding lanes and footpaths, and there are excellent books and local guides on sale in the village shops. Although the High Street, the Tye and the river paths are the main attractions, there is much more to Alfriston than at first meets the eye. This is a well populated and thriving community, ideally sited by its Saxon founder close to the river and sheltered by the wooded slopes of downland which rise above the village to the west.

Deans Place Hotel

Looking across the valley to Firle Beacon

10

THE VALLEY BETWEEN THE HILLS

Leaving Alfriston on the B2108, the road passes Deans Place Hotel on the southern outskirts of the village. Set now in beautiful gardens, the earliest record of a building on this site was in the twelfth century, when it was part of the Frog Firle estate, belonging to Wilmington Priory, and used as a 'pest house', or hospital for people with a contagious disease. In Tudor times it became a moated manor house, owned by the de Dene family. The property and the surrounding estate passed through the hands of many owners over the years until about 90 years ago it was sold in plots and ceased to be an estate.

Frog Firle

The road from Alfriston to Seaford is narrow and has some steep bends and turns as it approaches the hill of Hindover – an abbreviated version of the name High and Over. Above the wooded slope of Windmill Bank the stone tower of an old windmill, converted now to a private house, is surrounded by flint walls and a little further on Frog Firle house lies close to the road, above the river. The house, now a youth hostel, has the date 1538 over a window and until 1950 was the home of the Austen-Leighs, descendants of Jane Austen's family. The nearby Frog Firle farm-house was built in the sixteenth century on the site of a grange belonging to Wilmington Priory and a thousand years ago this was a place of some importance. In the Domesday Book the area, which reaches to the top of Hindover, was recorded simply as Firle, and had population double that of Alfriston. By 1288 the name was recorded as Frogge Ferle. The prefix of Frogge to distinguish it from other 'Firles' has perhaps come from its close proximity to the river and the thriving population of

From High and Over – 'one of the most breathtaking views in Sussex'.

The white horse of no great antiquity.

frogs in this area. A migration of toads and frogs occurs every spring and across the river at Litlington motorists are alerted by small signs warning 'TOADS CROSSING, PLEASE DRIVE SLOWLY'.

On the crest of High and Over there is a car park and a path through a copse which leads to the top of the steep side of the valley. From here is one of the most breathtaking views in Sussex, across to Windover and the Weald far beyond and to Litlington and the hills across the valley. Then, a little further along the path, out of the copse to the open hillside, is a long vista south to the sea, the light glinting on the wide meanders of the river.

Litlington

A footpath down to the valley and a little back tracking will bring walkers to a path below Frog Firle called Cow Lane, which crosses another White Bridge over the river to Litlington. In Saxon days this was the site of a tun, or homestead, owned by *Lytela,* whose nickname was 'the small one.' In keeping with the name inherited from its former owner Litlington is still small, and tucked snugly under the hill. The church stands on raised ground overlooking the river and the narrow village street has flint faced cottages and a good inn, the Plough and Harrow. Quiet it is, but alive. There are always people about and the tree shaded terraced tea gardens have been here for years, still providing a warm and sheltered place for refreshments in the open air.

Take the road south from here and you will see the white horse carved high into the hillside of High and Over. It has been there since 1838, and was cut again in the 1920s by a group of well wined friends after an evening at the Smugglers Inn in Alfriston. They made a good job of it for the 90ft long horse is well proportioned and well drawn. It had to be covered in the Second World War so that enemy aircraft could not use its white form as a navigation aid. It is now owned and cared for by the National Trust.

Charleston Manor

Following the valley road south but still within sight of the white horse, Charleston Manor lies on the left, set well back in a wooded coombe. This too was a site of Saxon settlement, and took its name from a social class of the time, Carl's tun. It was once linked to the river by a creek,

Charleston Manor and its twelfth century dovehouse.

which dried to become a bog, and has now been transformed into a tranquil lake. The manor house that is there today is described by Pevsner as 'a perfect house in a perfect setting'. The original manor was built by William the Conqueror's cupbearer. Later additions and alterations date from Tudor and Georgian times. There is a large stone dovecote in the garden which is still used by the local bird population for the purpose for which it was intended. It has 350 nesting holes but their occupants are not now destined to end up as delicacies for the table as would have been their destiny in earlier days.

Artist Sir Oswald Birley, who died in 1952, lived here and converted the 300 year old outbuildings into a long two storeyed residence, with a music room on the eastern end overlooking a walled garden. Today Charleston Manor is privately owned and the enduring beauty of the old house is set now in a magnificent garden sheltered from the winds by the surrounding woodland. Behind the house, overlooking a wide lawn, two great barns have been joined together to form one building. Music festivals are held in them at least once a year and here too, if you wish, you can have your wedding.

On the eastern side of the valley is Friston Forest – a modern woodland where planting began in 1927 to protect underground water supplies. It now covers more than 2,000 acres of downland. Fast growing conifers were first established to protect the beech and other broadleaved trees suitable for the area from the salt laden winds. As the pines and firs are gradually felled the forest will become mainly beech and after many centuries, on this part of the Downs, the process of forest denudation that begun in the Iron Age will have been reversed.

The royal estate of West Dean

Set deep in the forest West Dean was a Saxon royal estate. King Alfred was visited here by his biographer, Bishop Asser, late in the ninth century. He had travelled from Wales and in his account of the journey the bishop wrote:

'I arrived through great spaces of country, as far as the region of the Saxons . . . which in Saxon is called Suthsex'.

In later years West Dean was a large manor with a busy farming community. The flint faced buildings which stand here now and the barns which have been converted into

Flint, brick and tile hung cottages in West Dean.

homes bear witness to the days when there were 2,000 sheep on the hillside and fifty six draught oxen used for ploughing. There is a pond and a fine church with a tower capped by shingles, resembling a knight's helmet. Be warned that there is no parking for cars, but a walk up the road takes only ten minutes and there are well signposted paths leading to West Dean from the car parking areas on the edge of the forest.

The narrow road from Litlington now joins the busy A259 coast road and at the foot of the hill on the borders of Friston Forest is Exceat. A

The stone marking the site of the parish church of Excete, built in the eleventh century and abandoned in the fifteenth century.

river crossing has existed here for centuries and the raised path which runs along the south side of the main road was once a causeway, possibly dating from Roman times and used extensively in past centuries before a bridge was built. Long ago this region was an estuary and once there was a village here, high on the slope of the hills on the eastern side of the valley.

Exceat – the village that vanished

In the lower reaches of the Cuckmere some villages thrived, growing into towns, and some disappeared forever. The Middle Ages were turbulent times and though the pace of life was slow compared to today the passage of years could shift the balance of survival for many small hamlets and villages. Exceat was one that did not survive. The present spelling and pronunciation has been in use for many years but on old maps it appeared as Excete and was pronounced Eckset. This could have simply meant settlers by the Exe, thought to be the old British name of the Cuckmere, or even Ecci's settlement, from the Saxon era. In

1332 tax returns indicated the settlement had between sixty to 100 inhabitants and in 1913 the foundations of an early Norman church constructed of flint, chalk and malmstone were discovered.

The people who lived at Exceat were farmers and fishermen but a series of disasters, which included the climate swing known as 'the little Ice Age', followed by floods, and the bubonic plague which swept across Europe in the fourteenth century, caused their demise. The Black Death, so called because of the dark spots that developed from bleeding under the skin, was carried across the Channel by the rats that lived in the holds of ships. The terrible disease halved the population of Britain and that of Exceat and by 1460 there were only two houses standing and the church was in ruins. In 1538 the two remaining households in the parish were directed to look to West Dean for their spiritual needs. Today nothing remains of Exceat but the short aromatic grass on the hillside, home now to skylarks, and a stone erected by the Sussex Archaeological Society on the site of the old church.

The fortunes of the Cuckmere valley from Alfriston to the sea might have been very different if Exceat village had survived and prospered but fate took a hand and today the shore line of cliffs and the shingle beach at the mouth of the river are the only areas of undeveloped coastline between Hastings and Littlehampton.

Seven Sisters Country Park

From East Dean the road turns the corner at the top of the hill before descending to Exceat and it is from here that the view of the meanders snaking across the valley and the wide stretches of the Downs is at its best. At the foot of the hill, close to the junction of the road from Litlington, the old Exceat farmhouse lies a little back from the main road on the site of a former manor house. It is now a restaurant and tea garden and next to it is the Visitors Centre of the Seven Sisters Country Park. Taking its name from the high white chalk cliffs east of the river's mouth, this valued conservation area of 700 acres, owned by the East Sussex County Council and managed by the Sussex Downs Conservation Board, extends through the valley and includes downland on each side of the river's course from Exceat to the sea.

The footpaths over the hills and the easy walk on level ground to the beach at Cuckmere Haven have made this area a great attraction to both local people and holiday visitors. It never seems crowded, for groups of walkers are dwarfed by the width of the valley and the hills around it, but it is estimated that 450,000 people visit the park every year. Part of the valley walk has been concreted to make it suitable for wheelchair users, and for the more adventurous wheelchair users there is access over short grass in the lower valley to the beach. Each day subtly changes the scene, dictated by the weather and the tides. Sheep have been a feature of the Downs for centuries and they are still here today, grazing on the hills and around the meandering course of the old river path. The farm at Foxhole halfway to the beach, tucked into a fold of the hills, offers camping facilities for walkers but those who arrive by car can park at Exceat, either opposite the Visitors Centre at the foot of the hill on the A259, or in the car parks on the edge of the woodland behind the Centre. Maps are available of the footpaths in every direction and there are displays, books and leaflets about the social and the natural history of the area. There is a tactile map for the blind and visually impaired together with three different tapes. The rangers who patrol the park record each day's bird sightings on a noticeboard at the Centre. One day in October last year there were more than sixty species noted,

The Cuckmere flows quietly from Exceat through the country park

The Golden Galleon.

including gulls, waterfowl, herons, kestrels and owls, and the smallest British bird, the Goldcrest.

Sketches and photographs illustrate the incredible range of natural life, including the coastal reaches, with a map showing the different outlets of the river mouth since the eighteenth century. On display is part of a mammoth tusk found at Hope Gap, near Seaford Head, in 1993 embedded in deposits of an ancient river bed and reckoned to be 25,000 years old. Here too are details of the burial mounds, the round and long barrows of prehistoric man, one of which lies high on the field above the centre, and some fine examples of flint axe heads and arrow heads. Old farming implements and an ox yoke bring echoes of the more recent past.

On the other side of the river, across the bridge that takes the A259 west to Seaford, is the Golden Galleon. The original building was probably a small shepherd's bothy, part of the Chyngton farm estate until a marriage settlement in the 1750s separated the property, which came into the hands of Captain Ann of Drusillas in the 1930s. A bungalow was erected at the rear and it became a tea room and a half way point for the river trips from Drusillas. After the war there were caravan and camping sites at the Golden Galleon but these disappeared in the 1970s after new planning legislation for the area was passed. The Golden Galleon was purchased by Wheelers, the fish restaurant owners and later by the Courage brewery, which placed it under the management of Stefano Diella and his wife. They afterwards became tenant managers for the Fosters group and in 1992, with other family members, they became the outright owners.

The small (7ft 10ins by 15ft) brick building just above the car park houses the inn's own brewery of real ales. Alan Edgar, the head brewer, supervised the first brew in 1994. Since then the range has grown to include ten different types. Some are regular and some are seasonal beers and many have historical associations with the

The brewhouse of the Golden Galleon.

Cuckmere Valley. There is, for instance, Saxon King, with the head of Alfred the Great on the pump badge, and Saxon Berserker, a beer named after the champion warrior who traditionally headed the attacking force, armed with axe and shield, and no doubt well primed with the potent ale of the times. Other names include Cuckmere Haven Best, Guv'nor and Golden Peace. The latter, which has a logo of a dove flying over the Downs, was brewed for the fiftieth anniversary of VE Day. With a strength of 5.5% this is strong drink. It is known locally as 'Stress Control'. These ales are a speciality of the Golden Galleon but occasionally brews are ordered for organisations like the Campaign For Real Ales.

From the Golden Galleon the last part of the journey down the river valley has to be on foot.

Cuckmere Haven looking south from the old village of Excete.

11

A SHINGLE BEACH AND
SALT WATER

Paths head south from Exceat, one at the side of the cut and two others that follow the contours of the valley on each side. The footpath starting from the car park of the Golden Galleon leads directly to the western side of the river's mouth but also has a branch on the right to Chyngton and from there to Seaford Head. The eastern footpath is wide and easy, starting from opposite Exceat farmhouse and leading to the shingle ridge, passing close to the meanders and Foxhole farm.

Today this area is a walker's paradise but during the Napoleonic wars there was a battery near Exceat farmhouse where soldiers were stationed to repel an invasion if it came. During the Second World War Cuckmere Haven and the estuary had machine gun posts and tank traps

The Seven Sisters and, below, the beach at the foot of Haven Brow.

in strategic positions in readiness for invasion by Hitler's troops. Operation Sea Lion was to include a landing at Cuckmere Haven but fortunately, after the Battle of Britain in 1940, Hitler delayed this strategy and like Napoleon before him made the fatal mistake of invading Russia instead. A further use was made of the Cuckmere meanders at that time. Lights were placed across the width of the valley and were switched on at night if an air-raid was imminent to confuse the Luftwaffe bomber pilots into believing they were over the port of Newhaven rather than open country.

The eastern path passes a low cliff face by the layby on the concrete road and at the base of this vertical part of the bank are pieces of chalk and flint set in a series of U-shapes and fragments of chalk in fine mud. This is Coombe Rock, a relic of the last Ice Age when the South Downs had a very cold climate, only the surface thawing for a time in the summer months. This process loosened the surface chalk which moved down the slopes as the snow melted in a thick muddy porridge, to freeze again with the onset of winter. The lands around the Cuckmere then were bare and treeless, the river ran 80 feet below and herds of bison and reindeer roamed the hills and valley.

The Seven Sisters

The sea has since encroached far inland and the sheer white cliffs of the Seven Sisters, sculpted by wind and tide, rise steeply to the east of Cuckmere Haven. These lofty natural formations are seen to their best advantage from the paths which lead down from Seaford Head. Each has a name. From west to east they are:

1) Haven Brow, height 255ft
2) Short Brow, which is 214ft high
3) Short Bottom, which leads to Foxhole
4) Limekiln Bottom, the site of an ancient kiln
5) Rough Brow, 216ft high and covered with rough grass
6) Further Bottom and
7) Bran Point, height 160ft.

As the tide recedes from the beach a shallow shelf of chalk, rock and pools is revealed and the more sheltered northern side of the ridge is home to plants and flowers of the shingle habitat. Rare now, with a beauty uniquely their own, the yellow horned poppy grows here,

The former coastguard cottages overlooking the haven.

together with sea kale, bugloss and sea mayweed. Nature is in control now, right to the sea, but in 1939 the southern end of the valley was threatened with development. There were plans for a country club complete with brick chalets for 500 people. The outbreak of war put an end to the scheme and the land is now in the safe hands of East Sussex County Council.

Shipwrecks and smugglers

The haven is an exhilarating place to be when the sea runs high and the storm clouds scud across the sky in the darker days of winter. It was in weather like this in 1747 that a British ship, the *St Paul*, with a French privateer in pursuit, was sighted off Cuckmere Haven by fishermen. The *St Paul* rounded Beachy Head and kept inshore of the French ship but grounded on a sand bank.

A rowboat was seen to leave the privateer and another boat left the *St Paul*, carrying the crew and heading for the shore. The rumour spread fast that the cargo of the British ship was worth £20,000, and men ran to Seaford for muskets, powder and shot. Crowds gathered on the shore and thirty would-be rescuers put off in boats to the abandoned British ship, which had been boarded by the French. They met no resistance and secured the ship, but magistrates and Customs men arrived in time to make sure that the cargo did not go astray. However, after some lengthy legal ramifications, they had some reward. At the Old Tree in Seaford the owners of the stricken ship shared out £1,000 salvage money between eighty claimants.

On the western side of the haven the old coastguard cottages on the lower cliff are protected from the sea by concrete laid against the cliff face. The excise men and coastguards stationed there did their best but were often powerless to stop the well organised gangs of smugglers plying their illicit trade with France. Smuggling began in the fourteenth century when an onerous tax on wool was levied, and became a recognised industry in Sussex when further taxes were imposed on goods such as silk, lace, tobacco, tea and spirits. Fishermen and farm labourers aug-mented their meagre wages by helping the 'owlers', so named because their operations took place mainly at night, to move their contraband along recognised routes to ready markets in towns and cities. Cuckmere Haven and the river passage were ideal for the purpose and every one of the villages in the valley was involved. Secret rooms and under-ground passages were ready and waiting to conceal cargoes as the men beached their boats on the shore.

Although there were four coastguard stations between Beachy Head and Seaford the smugglers were quite open about their activities. A let-ter published in the Sussex Weekly Advertiser in 1783, states the case:

'There is a most convenient port, about a mile from Seaford, for smugglers to land their goods, and so daring are they become that a dozen or more cutters may frequently be seen laying-to in open day.

'On Tuesday evening between two and three hundred smugglers on horseback came to Cookmere and received various kinds of gifts from the boats, till at last the whole number were laden, when they went their way in great triumph.'

'A week before upwards of three hundred attended at the same place, and though the sea ran mountains high, the daring men in the cutters made good the landing and the men on horseback took all away.'

Trackways from Cuckmere Haven allowed the tub men who led the horses with barrels strapped across their backs, to head off to pre-arranged hiding places. The Alfriston Gang, led by Stanton Collins, was one of the most notorious in the area. He lived at Market Cross House, in Alfriston, now the Smugglers Inn, which had a wealth of passages and doorways, one room having no less than six exits. Many tales have been told about this legendary gang, one concerning a Dutch ship which was wrecked near the shore and said to have been emptied in two nights, despite heavy seas. The ship's lion figurehead was stolen as part of the loot and kept at the Market Cross House. It later appeared outside the Star Inn and is there to this day.

Although there was wide acceptance of smuggling the Customs and Revenue men saw the darker side. Some, it was true, accepted bribes to look the other way but many did try, against vastly superior and well armed numbers, to halt the illegal trade. Stanton Collins was finally arrested, tried, convicted and transported – not for smuggling but for sheep stealing and the last of his gang died in 1895 aged 94, in the Eastbourne workhouse.

Journey's end. The song of the birds of meadow and woodland has given way to the harsher cry of gulls wheeling around the cliffs as the Cuckmere meets the sea. A modest, quiet river, reflecting always the changing moods of season and weather, and rich with secrets from centuries past.

APPENDIX A

INNS AND RESTAURANTS	*Telephone:*
Three Cups Inn, Three Cups Corner.	01435 830252
Horse and Groom, Rushlake Green.	01435 830230
The Star Inn, Old Heathfield.	01435 863570
The Warbill in Tun, Warbleton.	01435 830636
The Jack Cade, Cade Street.	01435 865557
Blackboys Inn, Blackboys.	01825 890283
The Star, Waldron.	01435 812495
Clara's Restaurant, East Hoathly.	01825 840339
The Six Bells, Chiddingly	01825 872227
The Gun Inn, Horam.	01825 872361
The Yew Tree Inn, Arlington.	01323 870590
Horam Inn, Horam.	01435 812249
The May Garland, Horam.	01435 812692
The Homely Maid Restaurant, Hailsham.	01323 841650
Old Oak Inn, Arlington.	01323 482072
The Berwick Inn, (Adjacent to Berwick Station).	01323 871277
The Cricketers Arms, Berwick (Off the A27)	01323 870469
Giants Rest, Wilmington.	01323 870207
Wishing Well Restaurant, Wilmington.	01323 487967
The Sussex Ox, Milton Street.	01323 870840
Drusillas Restaurant, Alfriston.	01323 870234
Badgers Restaurant, Alfriston.	01323 870849
The Smugglers Inn, Alfriston.	01323 870241
The George, Alfriston.	01323 870319
The Star Inn, Alfriston.	01323 870495
The Wingrove, Alfriston.	01323 870276
The Plough and Harrow, Litlington.	01323 870632
Litlington Tea Gardens, Litlington.(April-Oct).	01323 870222
The Golden Galleon, Exceat Bridge.	01323 892247
Exceat Farmhouse Restaurant, Exceat.	01323 870218

HOTELS	*Telephone:*
Boship Farm Hotel	01323 844826
Deans Place Hotel	01323 870248
White Lodge Countryhouse Hotel	01323 870265

This list is far from complete and is for guidance only. It was correct at the time of writing but it is always advisable to telephone before making a long journey to a specific destination.

APPENDIX B

PARKING PLACES

There is parking for visitors at Michelham Priory, Abbots Wood, Arlington Reservoir and Wilmington Priory. There are two off road parking places (small) on the lower slopes of Windover Hill; two public car parks at Alfriston; one at Exceat, at foot of hill on east side; in Friston Forest; and three off the High Street in Heathfield.

There are others and roadside parking is acceptable if the road is wide enough but care should be taken not to cause an obstruction in narrow lanes.

FOOTPATHS

The Wealdway and the Southdown Way both cross the Cuckmere and there are many other paths, too numerous to list, in the region of the river. Ordnance Survey Landranger 199 or any of the many books and maps for walkers offer a variety of long, short and themed walks

OTHER SERVICES

Cuckmere Valley Ramblerbus - Berwick, through valley to Exceat, Seaford and return on circular route. Runs April to September serving the Cuckmere Valley community and walkers. This bus will stop to pick up or set down in the rural area wherever it is safe to do so. Hourly service on Saturday, Sunday and bank holidays only. Inquiries: **01323 870032**. To hire: **01323 848516**. Timetables and route map available at Tourist Information Centres.

Bike Hire – Cuckmere Cycle Co. At Seven Sisters Country Park, **01323 870310** and at Horam, Cuckoo Trail, **01435 813000**. Open all year. Closed Mondays, except on bank holidays and in the school holidays.

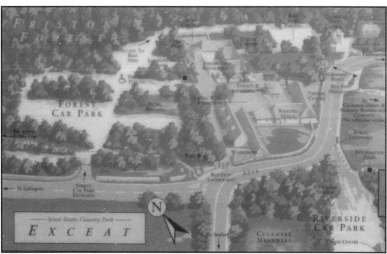

APPENDIX C.

LOCAL INFORMATION:
Eastbourne Tourist Information Centre, Cornfield Road, Eastbourne.
Tel: 01323 411400. Open 9.30 am-5.30 pm. Monday to Friday (all year).
Saturday. 9.30am-4pm in winter, 9.30am-5pm (summer) Sunday 10am-
1pm. (summer).
Wealden Tourist Information Centre, Boship Roundabout, Lower Dicker.
Tel: 01323 442667. Open 9.15am-5pm Monday to Friday. 10am-5pm on
Saturday and Sunday.
Seaford Tourist Information Centre, 25 Clinton Place, Seaford.
Tel: 01323 897426. Open 9am-5pm. Monday to Friday. 10am-5pm on
Saturdays in summer.
Michelham Priory, Upper Dicker, Hailsham. Tel: 01323 844224
Open 10.30am-4pm March to October; 10.30am-5pm in April, July and
September; 10.30am-5.30pm. Watermill normally open from 2pm but this
may vary.
Arlington Stadium, Hailsham. Tel: 01323 841642
Knockhatch Adventure Park, Hailsham. Tel: 01323 442051. Open
weekends and all school holidays between 1 April and 30 October from
10am-5.30 pm.
Drusillas Zoo Park, Alfriston. Tel: 01323 870234. Open all year, except
December 24, 25 and 26, from 10am-5pm. (summer) 10am-4pm. (winter).
English Wine Centre, Alfriston. Tel: 01323 870164. Wine shop, wine tast-
ing, museum, valley tours. Caters for weddings and private parties.
Open 10am-5pm all year except from 23 December to 2 January.
Clergy House, Alfriston. Tel: 01323 870001. Open 10am-5pm, April to
October. Closed Tuesdays and Fridays. Guided walks by National Trust
Countryside Wardens can be arranged here.
Seven Sisters Country Park Visitors Centre, Exceat. Tel: 01323 870280
Open from 10.30am-4.30pm on weekdays between April and October and
10.30am-5pm on Saturday and Sunday and bank holidays. Winter open-
ing: Weekends only 11am- 4pm from November to March.

BIBLIOGRAPHY

Alfriston Past and Present by W H Johnson, SB Publications, 1998
Almost a Gentleman by John Osborne. Faber and Faber, 1991
The Cuckmere, Another Sussex River by Edna and Mac McCarthy.
Lindel Publishing Company, 1981
Deanland ALG by Peter Waring. Published by Laughton Air Museum
East Sussex Inns by Brigid Chapman. Countryside Books, 1988
Exploring Alfriston and the Cuckmere Valley by Sandy Hernu.
S. B. Publications, 1996
Hailsham and its Environs by Charles A Robertson. Phillimore, 1982
The Handbook of British Archaeology by L Adkins and RA Adkins.
Macmillan, 1983
Heathfield Park by Roy Pryce, 1996
Hidden Sussex by Warden Swinfen and David Arscott. BBC Radio Sussex,
1984
The Iron Industry of the Weald by Henry Gleere and David Crossley.
Leicester University Press, 1985
Journey Through the Weald by Ben Darby, Robert Hale, London, 1986
Merrydown - Forty Vintage Years by Graeme Wright., Merrydown Wine plc,
1988
Scarecrows Legion by G Hufton and E Baird. Rochester Press, 1983
Steaming through East Sussex by Peter Hay. Middleton Press, 1985
Sussex Archaeological Collections
Sussex Place Names by Judith Glover. Countryside Books, 1997
Sussex Scandals by Rupert Taylor. Countryside Books, 1986
Sussex Women by Sharon Searle. Jak Books, 1995
Watermills of Sussex by Derek Stidder and Colin Smith. Baron Birch, 1997
The Wilmington Giant by Rodney Castleden, Turnstone Press, 1983
Wealden Iron by Ernest Straker, David and Charles Reprints, 1969

S.B. PUBLICATIONS publish a wide range of local interest titles
on Sussex and other counties in England. For a catalogue please
write to:
S.B. Publications, 19 Grove Road, Seaford, East Sussex BN25 1TP
or access our website on www.sbpublications.swinternet.co.uk